# Hermanisms

JOHN L. HERMAN JR.

Edited by Carmen Walsh

HSB Press

2007

Hermanisms

www.Hermanisms.com

Edited and designed by Carmen Walsh


ISBN-13: 978-0-9790204-1-4
ISBN-10: 0-9790204-1-7

Library of Congress Control Number: 2007921657

HSB Press
11615 Greenspring Avenue
Lutherville, MD 21093 USA
Herman@hsbpress.com

Distribution by Itasca Books
www.itascabooks.com

Printed in the United States of America

# Dedication

To a man who worked to give a better life to his children and grandchildren, my father ...

John L. Herman Sr.

"Poppy"

# ACKNOWLEDGMENTS

After *The Innkeeper Tales* was published, people kept asking me how I came to write a book. As a storyteller, my need to share had extended from gabbing with the closest person who would listen to producing a beautiful hardcover book that anyone could read. And the readers told me they liked what I had to say. So I would like to thank all of the people who encouraged my first work, for without them, this second book would not have happened.

I would also like to acknowledge the owners of independent bookstores who opened their doors to a new author and offered a small publisher the opportunity to showcase a book—because I've found out that writing a book is one thing and selling a book is another matter. In particular, I want to acknowledge the people at Greetings & Readings for their help in launching the *Tales*.

And then there are Carmen Walsh and Clarinda Harriss, two wonderful women of talent who are blessed with a work ethic and a dedication to help others achieve. They have been the backbone of my getting two books out in less than a year. Clarinda edited the first project with some assistance from Carmen. For this book, Carmen took the editing lead, but we still had Clarinda's guiding hand. And Carmen's design work gives me hope that even more people will pick up the books to learn what they are about.

Finally, I want to acknowledge the wonderful encouragement of my wife, Maggie, and my children, Kelly, Colleen, Shannon, Julie, and Sonny, who bring me positive energy and loving support.

# CONTENTS

## INTRODUCTION

We all love the stories about entrepreneurs that started with little or nothing, working from their homes, and then just a few years later found themselves trading on Wall Street. Reality check: the odds of this happening are about the same as getting rich by buying a lottery ticket. (Many people try both approaches—and still stay poor.)

In the United States, there are about six million small businesses.[1] Each year, more than half a million people decide to throw their hats in the ring and start their own companies. But in that same year, roughly the same number of companies give up and close their doors.[2]

Why? Here's one reason: **approximately 60% of businesses never make a profit.**[3]

Statistics say that if money is the driving force behind starting your company, you will lose. If money is your primary goal, you can work for someone else and get a paycheck every week. You won't risk losing any money, or your home, or the time you would need to spend trying to succeed when the odds say you will never make a cent.

So why do hundreds of thousands of people start a company every year?

Because they want the chance to succeed and are willing to pay the price? No.

**They do it because they want the chance to succeed and can't believe they will fail. It never enters their minds.**

If a high diver thinks he will hit the board, he probably will. If an athlete thinks he will fumble the ball, or miss the next pitch, or get tired near the end of the race, he probably will. So these individuals focus on thinking positively. Entrepreneurs are already programmed for a positive outcome: it's a character trait. And so many of them wake up a few years later, wondering why they made the leap.

**This book is intended to make you think. It's not intended to discourage you from starting a new venture. It is intended to make you realize issues you may want to ignore, but shouldn't— at least not if you want to be in the 40% that might actually make a profit.**

And this book has another goal: to make you understand that playing the game gives you more than just money. There are other "profits" to be derived from being your own boss. While your company may not make you rich, or last a lifetime, it will enhance your being—if you choose to let it.

## 1,000 Business Failures and I'm Still Standing

I'm a business failure expert. Not many people know as much about business failure as I do. And I'm eager to share what I have learned. But why should you listen?

In thirty-five years, I have owned more than twenty companies. One of them was a brokerage firm that engaged me to consult with over a thousand owners of financially troubled businesses. And in more than three hundred cases, we sold them, even though not one was making money.

That's right. **A thousand times I have sat in an office with a business owner and his lawyer or his banker to determine what, if anything, could be done to salvage the business or get the greatest return on the assets for the creditors.** And in all of those situations, the businesses were failing.

Each year, Dorsey Trailers sold trucks, flatbeds, and box trailers worth over $280 million. They had dealers all over the country. And they were millions of dollars in debt. My company, the brokerage firm that sold the assets in bankruptcy court, managed to sell a shut-down plant, with workers laid off, to investors who then reopened the plant. And other factories Dorsey owned were sold and continued their operations as well.

Thomaston Mills employed close to two thousand workers in five plants south of Atlanta and had worldwide annual sales of almost $300 million. They were going under. We sold their assets in bankruptcy court.

How about Superior Toy Company? They made the Mickey Mouse gumball machines that lived in seemingly every other house in America. And electric football and the hockey games with the moving metal rods to slide the players around. These were some of the most popular products in the country, but the company was losing money. It was sold in bankruptcy court. And my brokerage firm did the deal.

Mattison Technology too. And hotels and marinas and auto parts chains and metal stamping companies. Gun manufacturers turned into aerospace companies. Furniture makers, a mini-blind company, kitchen cabinet manufacturers… even Excalibur Automobile, a symbol of the excesses of the 1980s.

All of these companies at one time had made money and no longer did. Who would want these "dogs with fleas"? My brokerage firm must have had good salesmen, because we sold over three hundred of those dogs. All the sales were confirmed, in or out of a bankruptcy court, and settled transactions on which we collected a fee. We completed deals like this in forty-one different states.

With all the companies that I have owned and all those that I have consulted with and all those that my firm sold, I know something about business failure. The fact that I have built many successful enterprises to balance out the losers means I have received quite an education at the school of hard knocks. In fact, **I refer to the knowledge gained over all these years as my degree from the Herman School of Business.**

It's a degree that cost me a great deal of money, time, and pain to obtain. I value the knowledge from this degree more than if I had earned it at Harvard Business School. No disrespect to Harvard; it's a great school. If my grandchildren want to go there, I will help pay the tuition. My degree just happens to be one that I earned the really hard way. It cost more than Harvard's tuition. And it took many more "classes" than I would have had to attend at the Boston campus.

By reading this book, you can benefit from my years of experience in the real world of business.

The truths contained in these pages are not something you can learn in any college classroom that I know of—at least, not yet.

If you want to take the conversation past these pages, e-mail me at Herman@hsbpress.com. I'd love to hear from you.

The following pages contain axioms
born out of what was formed in my head
over many years.

Hence we have …

# HERMANISMS

Some are original ideas;
some express commonly known thoughts.
All are presented with anecdotal evidence of
their accuracy, drawn from my experience.

# Hermanism #1

**If owners calculated the time it would take them to succeed, most would never even try.**

If someone told you to walk across the park and one million dollars would be waiting for you on the other side, you would start putting one foot in front of the other. Half a million and you'd still start walking. One dollar and you might shrug and say no thanks. When you know what is on the other side of your effort, you make a conscious decision of whether it's worth it. Go or no go.

But what if I told you that the amount on the other side of the park was unknown, somewhere between one dollar and a million dollars? Every damn one of you would start hoofing it across the park. We make the effort only when we believe it will be worth it. But if we are unsure of the return, we tend to believe it will be the highest amount possible. Why is that?

As Americans, we are wired to believe we will always win. We'll always hit the game-winning home run. Always achieve the highest goals we set for ourselves. At least, that is what entrepreneurs believe. Like Pavlov's dog, we do what we are "supposed to do," believing there will be a treat at the end. And once we are programmed as entrepreneurs, even an occasional failure doesn't stop us from salivating at another chance.

That's why it is so important to let children experience both success and failure. Letting them win at a game just because winning makes them feel good—that's bullshit. Playing the game well enough to win is what makes us feel good. Knowing that they will not win every time is a healthy lesson. Too many kids are deprived of the opportunities to try and fail. Then, in adulthood, they flounder when they encounter their first real-life failure.

Now let's apply this Hermanism to your business.

What if you knew that working a hundred hours a week for about a hundred weeks in a row would result in your having bad health, problems at home, and a financial disaster on your hands? It happens to more than half of all businesses in America. Every other company started fails. In fact, 60% fail or close within six years.[4] That's right. Over half of all entrepreneurs will work endless hours and still fail. Remember, owning a business is not a walk in the park—where the million dollars might (or might not) be waiting on the other side.

Business is more of a workout. You wear out your body and mind, working endless hours under stressful conditions, sometimes without much support. When you do get to the other side, less than you expected may be waiting. In fact, sometimes at the other side is a little piece of paper that says "Pay up, sucker. You not only lost money; you owe money."

So why in the hell do we do it?

**Because we can't imagine we will fail.** We are confident that we will be in the minority that not only survive but thrive. **And for that chance, we'd walk through the park even if it was on fire.**

I have never spoken to a business owner who realized at the start how hard it would be. Or how much time it would take. And for many owners, it is one and done. Never again. Back to a job where someone else has the headaches of ownership and the responsibility for others.

**The true entrepreneurs shake the dust of failure off, wipe their hands clean on their pants, and look for what to get into next.** Somehow, to the true entrepreneurs, failing doesn't mean the game is over. It's just halftime, and they've got another chance to win as soon as the gun sounds.

# HERMANISM #2

## STUDY AND YOU SHALL LEARN.

My brother-in-law repeated this phrase to me countless times when I was young.

**You can't experience everything yourself.** It's a simple fact. You just won't live long enough to accomplish it all.

So you need to read and educate yourself about some things without actually experiencing them.

Learn sales techniques from a successful salesman. Learn bookkeeping from a CPA. Don't waste time trying to reinvent the wheel. Benefit from someone else's years of experience.

Go to a bookstore or library. Pick up any damn book you can find and study.

The simple effort of reading will put you ahead of those that don't read. For one thing, it allows you to learn from the mistakes of others before you make them yourself.

When I was young, there was a street saying among the inner city kids: "Stay in school and get a million bucks free." Even those little kids knew that what they could learn by reading and studying would get them further in life than those kids who never cracked a book.

# HERMANISM #3

## BUSINESS IS A CONTINUUM. SUCCESS IS THE CUMULATIVE GOOD RESULT OF RIDING OUT THE WAVES CRASHING AGAINST YOU.

One of the perplexities in business is figuring out what caused something to be successful. After all, it's only natural that we would like to do just what it takes to win—and cut out all of the unnecessary steps. So how do we figure out what those unnecessary steps are?

Let's look at my brokerage firm. We signed up companies in trouble and sold them, or their assets, to get the secured creditors their money back. For the deal to close, the creditors would sometimes have to take a loss. If they didn't take the loss, there was no closing. And no payday for us.

In my best year doing these types of deals, I made thousands of telephone calls and had about three hundred face-to-face meetings. I traveled four days a week and visited eighty new clients. But from those eighty new looks came only twenty-eight closings (i.e., paychecks). So why did I "waste" the other fifty-two visits?

Maybe I should have qualified some clients better over the telephone and saved myself some trips.

At the time, I was one of the best in the country at what I was doing. And I could not tell which trip was going to be successful and which one wasn't. Or which company we would want to work with and which one was a waste of time. If I couldn't tell and I was one of the best, surely the other less experienced partners at the firm couldn't accurately pre-judge which trips to make. But they certainly tried. They were always trying to figure out before the race was over what the outcome was going to be. Their thought process was this: Let's do only the sure things and always cash a check.

I, on the other hand, always traveled to get face to face with the bankers, so they could get to know me during a deal. That way, when I told them at the end of the day that they were going to have to take a loss, they would trust me that it was the right thing to do. It cost me about $800 to make some of those trips, and all I did was tell the banker something I could have said on the phone. So, thinking they were smart, some of my partners decided to call rather than fly. My closing rate on deals was 95%. Their closing rate was 50%.

**Which trips should I have skipped?**

You can't tell me with certainty which action in a string of actions that lead to a payday you can skip without sabotaging your success. Did the plane trip to introduce myself to the banker waste money? When I sent him a weekly report and then told him the same thing on the phone, was I wasting efforts? When I had bad news and went in person to deliver it, did it really matter that I made the trip?

How much work is enough to win the race? If you swim a hundred practice laps and win, should you cut down to ninety and see if you can still win? Or should you keep doing a hundred?

My philosophy was that shortcuts that might in fact work also might not—and therefore might not feed my kids. So I kept doing what had worked in the past; I never messed with success by trying to eliminate the "unnecessary" steps. And during my career with the brokerage firm, I had a higher closing rate than anyone else.

Let's talk about that constant wave against you. It can be a tough struggle, but sometimes you need the pressure against you to stay afloat. Try to fly a kite without the pressure from the wind against it; the kite will fall to the ground. You need something pushing you to keep working or you may just fall flat.

While it's hard work to fight that constant wave, fortunately, it is predictable to some degree. Payroll is due every other Friday. Supply bills have to be paid by the fifteenth. Rent is due on the first. This customer always pays his bill by the tenth. Some things we know and can plan on. And then some things just pop up and we have to deal with them.

We are told that, over time, good will overcome evil. Do what the Good Book says, and we'll land safely. Follow the tenets of good business, and profits will flow to our coffers.

I worked as hard in my failed ventures as I did in my successful ones. My failures were not for lack of trying. I was just as stupid in a win as in a loss. And just as smart in a loss as in a win.

There isn't one person I would trust to tell me what will fail and what will succeed. Cancer patients are told every day that they will die within a certain time period. Some die more quickly than predicted, while others live for many years. **There is a will in some human beings that cannot be measured.** And a force in the universe that we do not control.

We can't control all the outcomes, no matter what we do. But we can make the best cumulative effort of smart thinking, careful planning, great marketing, and recruiting the appropriate helpers—and then hope those efforts translate into a steady slow gain against the wave of reality pushing against us.

You can't see one step in the process and predict the outcome with certainty. So you better not skip any steps if you want the cumulative good to win the struggle.

And then, once in a while, things may come easy. You might step outside your car in the parking lot and find a hundred dollar bill. You might find yourself sitting in the plane seat next to a bigwig in your industry. You shouldn't expect it to happen, you don't deserve it to happen, but sometimes it does.

At a very young age, Eddie Murphy was working in clubs, making audiences laugh with his brash act. Rodney Dangerfield, another comic genius, was an old-timer by then. I read somewhere that Rodney saw Eddie perform early on, when Eddie was still an unknown. Not long thereafter, they ran into each other. Eddie had already become the biggest thing in the country. It had taken Rodney years to "get respect" and be a star. Rodney shrugged when he saw Eddie and said simply, "Who knew?"

# HERMANISM #4

## PEOPLE WHO RUN AROUND IN CIRCLES NEVER FIND THE FINISH LINE.

At some point, we have all been employees, working for someone else. And most of us have had at least one boss who seemed to live for wasting time. A boss who insisted on holding meetings to discuss every little thing. Who demanded countless reports about what we were doing or what we planned to do. And who never seemed to achieve anything of significance.

Make sure that what you are doing, and what you are asking others to do, is not busy work eating away at valuable time. Check that your activities are actually moving you closer to your objective. Spend your energy and that of your staff wisely. Don't have them running around in circles. Point them toward the finish line and show them how to get there.

Having checklists can be a good strategy. What do I need to do to get this plane off the ground and arrive at Point B safely? Have a checklist of the specific actions you need to perform. Do them and you are in the air, moving toward your destination.

# HERMANISM #5

## FIND A WAY TO CUT COSTS WITHOUT CUTTING CORNERS OR QUALITY.

Always put out the best product you can. Use the best packaging, the most attractive advertising. Always. Because even if people don't try your product, they will get an impression of it—and of you.

My first book was *The Innkeeper Tales*. The printer originally quoted the book at his cheapest price—with a low-budget paper cover. But I wanted a hardcover book. Ka-ching. I wanted an embossed hardcover book. Ka-ching, ka-ching. I wanted an embossed hardcover book in a sweet four-color dust jacket with the title gold foil stamped and embossed.

The printer cautiously answered: "You are going to spend about $3 more per copy doing it that way. This is your first book. What if it doesn't sell?"

If the book didn't sell, it was not going to be because I was worrying more about the cost than the quality of the product.

Regardless of the cover I chose, the book would have exactly the same words inside. But I felt a cheaper cover would change the message I was trying to convey. So I gave the book the first-class treatment I felt it deserved.

One reviewer had this to say: "One look at the book and you know that you've come upon an establishment that offers nothing but class." Scores of people have told me what a beautiful book *The Innkeeper Tales* is. How wonderful it feels in their hands. Book lovers know what I mean. Because of the extra money I spent on the production, even the people who haven't read a word yet are impressed with my work. And, in the long run, I believe the returns will justify the extra expense.

Unfortunately, I have a higher hill to climb with those returns because of another decision I made. I bought ten thousand postcards to promote the book; five thousand of them are still taking up space in my office. There's a cost I could have cut.

By the way, did you notice how nice the embossed gold foil stamping looks on this one?

# HERMANISM #6

## COST OF GOODS SOLD IS THE MOST COMMONLY MISUNDERSTOOD CONCEPT IN BUSINESS FAILURES.

Whether you manufacture a product, make food in a restaurant, sell a trinket in a retail store, or cut hair in a salon, I'll bet you can't tell me the real cost of the goods or services you sell. In over a thousand meetings with business owners, I have never heard one accurately state his cost of goods sold.

This lack of understanding sends more companies down the drain than any other single aspect of business.

Calculating the cost of goods sold is not as simple as adding the costs of the materials and labor, as many textbooks say. Getting to the true cost of goods sold is like figuring out a Rubik's Cube. You have to sift through a lot of data to know whether or not there will be a profit at the bottom line.

Let me give you a few examples.

## Manufacturers

I once owned a metal stamping operation that had won the bid for a major parts order. And we were losing pennies on each one of the thousands of parts going out the door. Why? Because the machine took longer to set up than we had anticipated, then didn't run as fast as we had calculated. So it made far fewer pieces per hour than we had estimated.

But the estimating department was finished its job. And now the parts order was in the manufacturing section, being filled. Those workers didn't know how many parts per hour had been estimated; they just stamped them out at their usual pace.

Weeks went by. Thousands of parts filled the bins that were then trucked to the buyer—who, by the way, was constantly hassling us to lower the price, because the customer they were making a finished product for was constantly hassling them. "What's another two cents per part going to do, break you?" was the battle cry of the buyer. "If you will just cut the price by two cents, we will double our order."

This order was for thousands of dollars' worth of parts, and the CEO was always looking for more sales. Our salesman saw a way to make the CEO happy. He cut the price and doubled the order. So now we were losing even more money per part—on twice as many parts.

In a large company, you don't catch up with these things right away. You may not find out that you are losing money for weeks or even months. If you make a hundred different products, as we did, you may not realize which product is causing the loss. And if you don't find the answer soon enough, you can hit the tipping point going the wrong way.

## Restaurants

All restaurant-goers—that is, all but the true "foodies"—have a certain threshold of cost that they will not cross. No matter how heavenly the meal, diners will pay only a certain amount higher for "top quality" than they would normally pay for an item. Price it too high and they will not order it.

Many chefs consider one particular brand of pork to be the best in America. Raised in California, the meat is tender and sweet. Pork from the local market can be good, but usually not this good. So, right off the bat, the per-pound cost is higher because of the unique nature of the product.

The chef in this story was always conscious of food costs. He knew he had to keep the cost of the food item to about 30% of the menu price, or he would lose money on the dish. So he calculated the cost of the pork and the other ingredients on the plate. He tripled that amount and put the price on the menu. It was steep—but the pork was indeed heavenly.

How good was it? It was featured in *Bon Apetit,* because one of the magazine's writers happened to eat in the restaurant while the pork was on the menu. This was the Holy Grail for the chef: to have his dish written about in the "Food Bible." After the article ran, the guests came in droves.

However, while many more guests were eating the pork, there didn't seem to be a correlating increase in profits. In fact, profits seemed to be going down.

I consulted with the chef on how he arrived at the menu price for the pork dinner. It didn't require more time to prep. Or more labor. Yes, the cost per pound was more, but the chef had accounted for that by setting the menu price higher than that of a normal pork dish.

I asked him where he got the pork. It wasn't delivered by a local purveyor; it arrived by Federal Express. At a cost of about $6 per serving.

The chef had not factored the shipping cost into the cost of goods when he decided on the selling price. And so, not only did each guest enjoy the best pork meal of their lives; the restaurant was paying $6 per person for them to do so.

## Retailers

Everyone who wants to be a retailer can approach a wholesaler and buy goods to sell. The free marketplace lets you set up shop in almost any financial environment. Corner stores in the ghetto sell some of the same products as the most expensive malls in America—and for less.

So why don't we all run down to the inner city and save ourselves some money? Because we are willing to pay more than just double the raw cost of goods for other considerations. Like the convenience of a store near our home or close to other shops we want to visit. In a cleaner and prettier environment. We shop where we want, and we pay different prices for the same products depending on where we buy them.

In some cases, if you, as a retailer, buy a larger quantity from a wholesaler, you can get a price break. And you can pass that price break on to your customers—because you have an edge over the competition on the raw cost of the product.

If you can make your store just pretty enough and just convenient enough and get that price edge in a big way, you can always sell your products at a lower price. Sears did it for almost a hundred years. Kmart shot to the top for a while. Now Wal-Mart leads the way.

Wal-Mart sells just about every item a person could ever need—and at a lower price than any mom and pop operation could ever offer. And they don't need wholesalers to do it; they go straight to the manufacturers. They almost always control a manufacturer's operations, by placing orders that dwarf those of all its other customers. And they get bare bones prices too. They want to sell whatever the manufacturer makes at the lowest price in America.

If you're a retailer, how do you compete with that?

By selling the unique items, not the items for the masses. By carrying high-end products. Even Wal-Mart can't carry everything. No store is that big. By being in a more convenient location. By having a nicer atmosphere.

Remember, customers want their product, but they are willing to pay more for it if their other needs are met.

## Service Businesses (Beauty Salon)

At a talk I gave not long ago, one of the attendees came forward to say that she had started a beauty salon, but was having difficulty making it. Would I please stop by to offer her some ideas? She even half-joked that she hoped I wouldn't tell her to just close the doors and quit. (She had just learned that I had said those words to other owners of failing businesses.) This salon was her dream: she desperately wanted it to succeed.

So I went to her salon. It was beautiful: professionally appointed, with attractive product displays and murals painted on the walls to make you feel like you were looking outdoors, as there were no real windows to the outside. The massage room was comfortable, with a gorgeous tiled shower. It looked like the place couldn't miss. So why wasn't she making enough money?

One challenge she would have to overcome was her location. The salon was not in a strip center for passing traffic to see. It was not in a shopping mall with foot traffic to catch walk-ins. It was on the second level of an office building, which was not yet fully occupied. But that could be overcome with some creative marketing.

My prediction is that she will make it. It's just that the threshold where she will realize a real profit is higher than she expected it to be—because she didn't really understand her cost of goods sold. To illustrate my point, let's examine a few items.

Most beauty salons buy products wholesale and then double the cost to sell them to their customers. Shampoo that costs the salon $2 is sold for $4. So that means if the salon owner sells $5,000 of products, she is making $2,500 profit. Right?

What about the cost of the space? If she pays $4,000 monthly rent and another salon pays $2,000 for the same amount of square footage (and the ability to service the same number of customers), doesn't it cost more for her to sell each product because her rent is higher? Yes. So, all other things being equal, she has to charge higher prices for the same services and the same products, or sell twice as many as the other salon, or she isn't covering her higher rent.

Let's look at the situation from another angle.

The salon is now operating at half capacity and falling just short of making money each month. So close to making money, but slowly going backwards. The owner needs to bring in just $3,000 more a month to break even, and after that she reaches the honey pot of profits.

My suggestions of how to increase revenue initially stunned her.

First, I suggested she sell products at half price with any service on Tuesday. Half off? That was her profit, and I had already showed her it wasn't enough. But, I pointed out, Tuesdays she was booked at only about 20%. It was almost a wipeout day for customers. If the products were discounted, maybe a few people would start coming on Tuesdays. So, while she was "giving away" the products, she would be making money from the additional customers.

The next thing I did was show her that the masseuse was killing her financially. The price of a massage at her salon wasn't any higher than at other salons; pricing wasn't the problem. She just hadn't realized a big enough book of clients yet to cover the cost of offering the service.

Within eyesight of the salon's office building were many more office buildings—and two major hotels. I suggested she offer certificates to the concierges for hotel guests to receive massages at half price. Again the salon owner was startled. How could she make money if she charged half the price?

I explained: Because there were no customers now. Getting half of the price of a massage was better than getting none of the price of a massage. You see, the main cost of a massage is labor. The salon owner was paying the masseuse to stand around and do nothing. And she was getting nothing back to help her bottom line.

What is the real cost of your service? There are many variable costs to consider: things like insurance, power and light, telephone, advertising, accounting services. What does it really cost you to provide that service? Are your prices covering your costs?

# HERMANISM #7

## YOU GO UNTIL YOU HIT A WALL. THEN YOU CLIMB OVER IT, DIG UNDER IT, OR GO AROUND IT. WHEN ALL THESE EFFORTS LEAVE YOU STILL BEHIND THE WALL, WALK AWAY AND DO SOMETHING ELSE.

**Any further effort in that endeavor is a waste of what you have learned and keeps you further from success at the next thing.**

We've all heard sayings like this. As I mentioned earlier, I do not claim to be the originator of all of the thoughts in this book. I am the product of my environment, as everyone is. Someone told me that this particular idea comes from the Bible. Maybe that's where I heard it first. Regardless of where it came from, it's an important lesson.

**When I look at successful people, they all seem to follow a similar pattern: lots of attempts and some successes.** How did they know when to stop something that wasn't working and try something else? What if they waited just one more week? Would their failure turn into a win? Where did they get the ability to let go of that paralyzing fear of "what if …" and move on?

**When should you give up?**

Only after you have done all that is in your control can you say that you have really tried at something. Then if you move on, you are not doing it because you are tired. Or scared. Or no longer have the same energy as you had when you started. You are moving on because it just won't work. Because there is nothing left for you to do to try and make it work.

Is there something else you can try? Call on more potential customers? Work another hour each day? If there is more that you can do, but you don't do it and quit, how will you know whether the failure was your fault or beyond your control? Remember, you will have to live with yourself after you fail. Will you look back and say, "I should have tried…"?

**To be a successful entrepreneur, you must feel satisfied with your own efforts.** Your goal should be to do everything within your control to make your project work. Do all of those things. Then if the project can't go any further (for reasons beyond your control), you don't have to beat yourself up when you close that door and move on.

Sure, you wanted to put out a hit record. Or make the Major Leagues, or have the best retail store or manufacturing plant or restaurant. But that goal was something that included two aspects: things you could control and things you could not.

If you built a club in New Orleans and it opened to rave reviews the night before Katrina hit, but then the floods washed everything away, you could say the club failed. But it failed because of something beyond your control. Failure hurts regardless of the reason, but you will heal and move on to something else much faster if you can't blame yourself for the failure.

But don't think that means a failure isn't your fault. You have to take the blame ultimately. In every Super Bowl, one team wins and one loses. Somebody has to take responsibility for the loss. Maybe the lineman didn't hold out the defense long enough. Maybe the quarterback underthrew the receiver. Maybe, and most often, it's a series of events. Mistakes happen. We are humans, after all.

When I fail, I always review what happened. And I take the appropriate blame. But I am hard on myself only if I didn't put the effort in to make it work, if I didn't do everything within my control. I can live with being wrong; I can learn from that and move on. And maybe I'll get the next one right.

# HERMANISM #8

## VIEW THE KNOWLEDGE FROM SOMETHING THAT FAILED AS THE PROFIT FROM THAT EFFORT.

My first business venture was to provide copying and secretarial services for doctors, lawyers, and other professionals. One day, a salesman came into the copy shop and asked if I would put up a display of the laminated plaques he manufactured. That way, our customers could order the mounting of their diplomas and other documents through us.

The display he had brought with him was wonderful. He hooked me right away. I asked him if we could use my personal documents in our display. My Certificate of Aeronautical Rating (Air Force Wings) went up, my college degree, the photo of my first solo ride in a jet. The plaques were awesome! I spent a few hundred dollars, but those plaques sure looked great on my wall.

Sure enough, our customers loved the plaque display. They began to bring in their materials to be put on plaques. Once a week, their documents were picked up, and a week later the plaques were delivered. We made money just for taking the orders. That plaque guy's setup intrigued me.

Then another salesman came in and sold me a machine that would stuff envelopes, wet the seals, and then close and stamp the envelopes. I loved that machine. It gave me more business. And the salesman loved my shop because I was making money as a mostly absentee owner. He liked what I did, and I liked what the plaque guy did.

Bing botta boom. I sold my copy shop to the envelope machine salesman, and I bought the plaque business. It was going to be my first venture into manufacturing. But I didn't rush in … no sir.

I was a business owner with a degree in business administration. I was no fool. I knew I needed to do some research, something called due diligence. So, before plunking down money to buy the plaque business, I flew to Colorado to see the guy who sold the laminating equipment—to make sure that people really were making money with these things. You weren't going to fool this boy.

In Denver, I saw an amazing operation. People swirling about offices. A line of machines humming with the plaque business. I looked out the window and saw Mile High Stadium. I was convinced.

I flew back to Baltimore, wrote the check, and went into the plaque business. How could it miss?

With the purchase, I acquired a shop: 1,500 square feet of space. It had an explosion-proof fan. And a paint spray booth. And a large saw to cut four-by-eight sheets of fine wood down to the plaque sizes. It had a laminating machine. And a showroom with gorgeous samples for customers to see when they came to drop off their documents.

I didn't know squat about this business, but it seemed sweet. Almost everyone had something that should (or could) be on a plaque.

I even took two partners for the ride. One cut his fingertip off the first night. (He was left-handed, and the saw guides were set up for a right-handed worker.) We didn't see him again.

And about that beautiful showroom. The customers never came. My strongest memory of the showroom is that the remaining partner and I played a lot of pinochle there. After a few weeks of that, we figured maybe we better go out and open up some accounts, to try and get some business.

Within a few weeks, we had opened fifty-five accounts. Fifty-five places that displayed our plaques and took customer orders for us. That meant fifty-five stops each week. I wore out a beautiful Buick Riviera driving hundreds of miles every week, picking up documents and delivering plaques. Even back then gas wasn't free, and that old Riviera barely got eight miles per gallon.

Plus there was the time at the shop to manufacture the product. Time to go buy supplies. And, oh yeah, time to do the paperwork that always seemed to be piling up.

Soon we had a steady flow of documents to make into plaques. We paid for the raw materials. We did the work. We picked up and delivered for free. And we finally learned how much it cost us to produce something that we sold for $10.

Ouch. Now you know where Hermanism #6 came from. I learned the cost of goods sold lesson the hard way.

Two years after buying the plaque business, we cried uncle and sold it. For one-third of what we had paid.

Ah, but the lessons learned were priceless.

# HERMANISM #9

## ARE YOU USING THE PH.D. YOU GOT FROM THE SCHOOL OF HARD KNOCKS?

Slow down a minute and think. Think about all the things that life teaches you every day.

Some lessons we learn the hard way—when bad things happen to us. And sometimes we get to learn them the not-so-hard way—when they happen to someone else and we are close enough to observe.

Of course, watching someone else's experience doesn't make nearly as much of an impression as experiencing it ourselves. So, as we get older and experience more of life, we should get wiser.

**For every business deal I did, I got more than money. I got an education.** About someone's style of negotiation. About a new way to look at financing. How to pull a balance sheet and income statement apart. A new tax angle.

And sometimes my read of the people or the problem was wrong. And I paid for it. Life's lessons seem to be magnified when our money is on the line.

Most people make only a few purchases in life that are so significant that they can be life-altering. Take the wrong job, and at worst you quit and get another one. Buy the wrong company, and they may come take your house.

**Learn what life is trying to teach you.**

# HERMANISM #10

## TRUST YOURSELF.

If you can't trust yourself, you shouldn't be an entrepreneur. You should be a worker and let someone else make the decisions.

At the end of the day, you have to live with your decisions—good and bad. If you screw up, at least you did what you thought was right.

# Hermanism #11

## If the ball lands in the rough, hit it from the rough.

You drive the ball three hundred yards straight down the middle of the fairway. Booya. Then, oops, on your next tee shot, the ball goes goober right (in honor of my friend Danny who always goes "goober right"). Now you're in the rough.

When the ball is in the rough, you have to change your thinking on the next shot. You have to recognize that the grass is higher here than on the fairway; that a tree limb is smack dab in your line of sight to the flag; that you are standing on the side of a hill, which means you need to change your stance.

**When things go wrong, you have to adjust from your normal course of action.** You have to think about where you are, not where you wanted to be. And there will be a ripple effect from all the changes you are making. Usually the guy in the rough gets a five or six, and the guy in the middle of the fairway makes par. And the first guy spends the rest of the round trying to catch up.

In golf, there is something jokingly referred to as a "foot wedge"—when you see the ball in the rough and you kick it (with your foot) out to the sweet grass of the fairway. And then you hit the green and still claim par. It doesn't work. You will get caught. You can't escape the reality of your situation by cheating.

It requires sharp thinking to scramble out of the rough and still make par. Perhaps taking an approach to the green that isn't quite normal, but might yield you a five instead of the six staring in your face.

There will be times when your business is in the rough. Maybe the inventory you have doesn't match the orders you are getting. Maybe the delivery date doesn't fit your schedule. When this happens, slow down your thinking. Plan a few options to get back to the fairway. Weigh those options. Imagine each outcome. Do not exacerbate the situation with another bad shot or another bad decision.

Trying a one-in-a-million shot—going through the tiny hole in the tree, slicing the ball around the corner, and then having it roll up on the green— often ends up with the ball smacking the tree squarely and almost taking your eye out when it ricochets back at you. And you end up still in the rough, but farther from the green than you were before. Yes, I have seen Danny take that second shot many times. He has seen me do it too. And it never works.

Don't count on a miracle to get you out of a crisis. Your business needs sensible thinking and a steady hand. Recognize that you are in the rough. Then plan the right move to get yourself out of the rough and back on course.

HERMANISM #12

## NOT KNOWING YOUR REAL MARGINS CAN KILL YOU.

During the early days of "doing deals" at my brokerage firm, my staff was rather unsophisticated. This anecdote illustrates just how unsophisticated.

We produced a term sheet on each deal with vital information: data about gross sales, types of assets, property descriptions, and so on. We would mail several thousand of these term sheets out, hoping to intrigue potential investors enough to call for more detailed information.

Many people did call. One such potential investor called and asked, **"What are the margins in this deal?"** The staff member who had answered the phone took out a ruler and measured the margins around the data on the term sheet. She replied, "About an inch on the right and an inch and a half at the bottom."

Once the caller had stopped laughing, he asked to speak to someone who actually knew something about the deal. So this is your bonus lesson: Never allow lower-echelon staff to answer questions from someone inquiring about a significant business matter. They could make you look ridiculous.

Onto more serious matters. Let's review some basic business principles, rules that apply in every situation.

The free marketplace will not allow you to have outrageous margins on any product or service. When others see that high profits can be made, the competition flows in. And then everyone has to lower prices to stay competitive.

If you sell pizzas for $20 and get away with it, others will soon be out there at $18, and so on and so on. Last week, I saw an ad: three pizzas for $15. You better be good and efficient, and sell a hell of a lot of pizzas if you are only getting $5 a pizza. You better know your margins.

Margins are not calculated just by taking the selling price of a product and subtracting the raw costs of materials and labor. You have to consider all of the other cost factors as well.

This can be as simple as one employer having union labor, where everyone makes the same wages, and another having a non-union shop, where he can fluctuate the wages against production with the same amount of people. Less cost, larger margin.

Margins can also be affected by borrowing habits. For instance, one manufacturer owns his inventory outright and never borrows money against it. He has no "interest per piece" cost. Another manufacturer pays 10% interest on the money that is borrowed against his inventory. Going a step further, one company keeps his accounts receivables, while his competition borrows against them. Boom, another 10% cost. And again, less margin.

If all else is equal (and it never is), then the company that doesn't borrow has a better profit margin.

It always amazed me when a company would load up with debt and owe 10% on millions of borrowed dollars while the competition stayed out of debt and beat his brains out on price. After all, the debt-free company can give away half the money the debt-laden one is paying in interest and still make a bigger margin.

And so we move on to Hermanism #13.

# HERMANISM #13

**DEBT IS A DESTROYER. IT IS THE WORST CANCER IN YOUR FINANCIAL LIFE, BE IT PERSONAL OR BUSINESS.**

Perhaps the most extreme example I know of for how debt can kill a business is a window fashion company my firm once sold.

At that time, the window fashion industry consisted of many small companies that made custom-sized window blinds. Gone were the days of heading to Sears and picking up one-size-fits-all Venetian blinds or Roman shades.

These new companies would take the measurements from your windows and custom-make mini-blinds for you in a variety of colors and styles. And they would deliver the blinds to the store where you purchased them. Suddenly, stores that sold wallpaper and paint could add a new department and sell a higher-end product, something that customers were willing to pay a higher price to have. There was an explosion in the industry: finally, customers could get the exact size blinds they needed in precisely the colors they wanted.

Now, to pick out the correct colors and cut the blinds to size, there was no automated assembly line of machinery in a factory. In fact, there was very little equipment required. The blinds were assembled by hand. It was cheap labor.

Dozens of such companies quickly appeared. Mom and pop could set up in the garage with a few supplies—voila, they were in business. Nothing distinguished one company's product from another's. All of the raw materials, including the slats and frames, came from just a few suppliers. And the large retailers knew it. They wanted an operation that could produce a consistent product, delivered in days.

## Purchase Debt

This particular company was started by two brothers. They decided to move their operation into a larger facility, one that could hold three hundred workers instead of thirty. They made the blinds in exactly the same way as mom and pop were making them in the garage; they just had a bigger garage.

Mom and pop couldn't keep up with the large retailers' high volume of orders, but the brothers could. Boom. Within just a few years, they went from a handful of small orders to $50 million a year in sales. Of blinds that were almost entirely handcrafted by cheap labor.

By then, the brothers had the economies of scale all businesses try to obtain. By being the biggest player in the marketplace, they could buy the large quantity of raw materials they needed at the lowest price. By shipping multiple orders to the same stores, they could save on shipping. Those advantages gave the brothers a hefty annual salary and the company still made $1 million a year in profit. That's $1 million a year in profit on a $50 million company. But they hadn't hit the lottery just yet. That was about to happen.

It seems that some investors wanted their $50 million a year business, with the $1 million profit. The investors were convinced that they could grow it ten times the size and make it a $500 million company. So they bought the company with $2 million cash down and $40 million of debt.

For the brothers, it was Harley Davidson city and see you down the highway. For the new owners, it was welcome to the insane world of overpaying for a company and adding so much debt service that survival was impossible.

**At 8% debt service, they needed $3.2 million a year just to pay the interest.**

**So at the current operating level, they were insolvent on the day they bought the company.**

Why would you put up $2 million of your own money for a company you immediately made bankrupt? Chutzpa? Greed? An exaggerated notion of your ability to increase sales by ten times—when every major retailer was already selling your product? Where was the growth going to come from?

Suffice it to say that within two years, the company was sold through a foreclosure, and the new guys paid many millions less than the secured creditors had loaned. A side note: The secured creditors also failed shortly after this transaction. They had made many of these speculative loans, hoping to become one of the largest asset-based lenders in America. What they achieved was being one of the largest asset-based lenders in America ever to fail.

*Epilogue:* The blinds operation was sold to a major window fashion company, for the appropriate price, in 1993. In the spring of 2007, I was walking through a big box store and saw the brand was still on display. The company that had bought the operation structured the deal properly and is still making money on the product line fourteen years later—in part, because they didn't overpay and overload the company with debt.

## Operating Debt

What about operating debt? Not just overpayment for a company, like in the previous story, but ongoing debt.

Consider this scenario: You make widgets. There are ten companies like yours making the same widgets. You all have the same production equipment. You all pay about the same cost for raw materials because your operations are almost the same size. This leaves three components that determine how much money you make versus your competition: (1) labor, (2) rent/mortgage, and (3) debt.

You all have the same labor costs, so no one has an advantage there.

Eight of the widget companies, including you, are operating out of inexpensive 1950s-style factories. Two newcomers prefer exotic-looking facilities—which do nothing for the product, but serve the company owners' egos. Those two owners trade their profits for real estate.

Ah, but debt. Six of the companies have no debt. They never borrowed money, and they always paid their bills on time. What was left was theirs, not a penny for the bank. You are, unfortunately, one of the other four. You owe money to the bank—

for borrowing against your inventory and your accounts receivables.

You've been keeping up just fine. But then the economy turns down just a tweak and your sales are weaker than expected.

Keep in mind, you don't make your profit on the first dollar of sales; you make your profit on the last dollar of sales. You can't make a profit until all of your costs are paid. **And debt is a cost.**

So, when the sales squeeze comes, the companies without debt can survive. Not so those with debt. You want a paycheck every week and the bank you owe wants a payment every week. Someone has to lose when the economy falls. If you decide to keep taking your check and skip the bank payment, you may win temporarily, but the bank will always win in the long run.

**It's not that your company isn't making any money. It's just not making enough money to pay both you and the bank.**

That's when my company would be called in to sell you out so the bank could get its money back. **Interestingly enough, I never sold a company that had no debt. Never got one call for that type of company.**

HERMANISM #14

## IF YOU DEFINE SUCCESS AS GIVING IT YOUR BEST EFFORT, YOU CAN BE SUCCESSFUL EVERY DAY.

This morning, I got out of bed expecting to write two thousand words for this book. I intended to contact my distributor for help with a bookstore question. I had to attend the funeral of a friend's mother. I wanted to finish negotiating the contract terms of selling one of my companies. I also planned to eat three meals, read the paper, watch some television, and do some paperwork.

At the end of the day, if I've done all of those things on my mental To Do List, I am satisfied. Sure, it would be nice to accomplish all of the long-range goals those immediate actions are intended to achieve, but that brings into play other people and their actions—and I can't control them. **I consider it a success when I have done all I can.**

In my brokerage firm days, after I had made a presentation on a deal, my partners would all ask me how I felt. How did it go? I always felt the same: great. I had done everything I planned to do. I was well prepared. I had represented our company well.

I felt successful because I did what I set out to do: give a good presentation.

Of course, getting the deal would make me very happy. It was the ultimate goal after all; it was why I put myself in those situations, to get as many deals as possible. But my feeling of success came from doing my part. I knew it was a numbers game and if I did my best enough times, the deals would come.

In some years, I made sixty such presentations. I lived through lots of long flights and rental cars, hotels and meals alone on the road, away from my kids. And only about twenty deals would get signed. Should I be happy only those twenty days a year? Or should I be happy every day, because every day I was giving myself a chance to get to those sixty meetings which would result in those twenty signed deals? Call me crazy, but I prefer to be happy more often than twenty times a year.

**Define success as accomplishing the little goals that will give you a chance at the bigger goals. And you can feel good about yourself every day.**

# HERMANISM #15

MILTON HERSHEY FAILED SEVERAL TIMES
BEFORE HE CREATED THE HERSHEY BAR.
IF THIS IS YOUR FIRST FAILURE, YOU MAY
HAVE ONLY A FEW MORE TO GO.

Most Americans by the age of ten have tasted a Hershey's milk chocolate bar. As a chocolate lover, I consider it absolute perfection. In pilot school years ago, we used to joke that a fighter pilot's breakfast was a Hershey bar and a Coke. Two American food icons.

But the Hershey bar wasn't the result of Milton Hershey's first try. He failed at his first confectionery in Philadelphia. He failed again in Chicago. And in New York. Family, friends, and investors were losing money and losing faith. Hershey never intended to fail and lose other people's money, but he did.

When Hershey returned to his home near Lancaster, Pennsylvania, he vowed to pay back his creditors. When you lose, realizing that you let others down, not just yourself, makes it hurt that much more.

So Hershey kept trying. He made caramels, like so many other candy makers, but he had always been fascinated by chocolate. And the Hershey bar was finally born.

With his success, Hershey was able to become one of the most famous candy makers in the world. He also became one of the greatest entrepreneur-turned-philanthropists. Because in addition to stick-to-itiveness, Hershey possessed another trait common among entrepreneurs: that when they finally hit the big time, they often want to share their success with others.

To a real entrepreneur, it isn't about making money. It's about winning. Being right about your idea. Seeing the realization of your dream. The money is great, and is something you can share, but it doesn't offer nearly the same satisfaction as accomplishing your goals.

Don't quit on your goals because you didn't achieve them the first time around. Pick up a Hershey bar and give it another go.

# HERMANISM #16

## SOMEONE IS BETTER AT IT
## THAN YOU ARE.

There is only one number one, only one best at anything. Thankfully, we live in an environment where even the tenth-best or the hundredth-best business may make some money. But why not try to learn something from the leaders?

Set aside your ego. Recognize that someone may be better than you are at what you do. Admit it—and then set your sights on becoming even better.

Who else makes what you do, sells what you do, or provides the same service you do—and is more successful at it? If you don't try to understand what they are doing better, you don't really want to win.

You see, another business fact is that sometimes number one slips and becomes number two or number three. Find a competitor that is more successful than you. Identify what they do better, combine that with your strengths, and then work harder or smarter. And maybe, just maybe, you'll be number one someday.

# HERMANISM #17

## "HOW MUCH MONEY DO I NEED TO MAKE THIS WORK?" USUALLY THE ANSWER IS MORE THAN YOU HAVE. DO YOU STILL WANT TO PLAY?

Gambling is about money management—and emotional management. Play Twenty-One in any casino and you will soon understand this.

Danny and I loved going to Atlantic City. Now, Danny is a good gambler. He is disciplined and smart, understands the mathematics of the cards, and holds his emotions in check. Usually. One night, he lost it. Of course, I thought his meltdown was hilarious. I suppose it wasn't so funny from his point of view.

In the game Twenty-One, a dealer "breaks" or goes over 21 about 28% of the hands. So, if you get 20, you are almost always going to win. On this particular night, Danny had two tens and he was smiling. The dealer was showing a five—an almost certain bust hand. A few cards later, boom. The dealer had 21.

Not discouraged, Danny smiled and said, "It happens" and "Every dog has his day." By the time these words left his lips, Danny had two more tens in front of him. "Here we go," Danny purred as the dealer showed a six. When the cards tumbled over and the dealer showed another six, giving her a total of 12, Danny clapped his hands and smiled. First a deuce was turned over and then an ace, giving the dealer a total of 15. Then another ace. Now she had 16. Almost certain death. When the five rolled over giving the dealer 21, she chirped with glee. Not a good thing, as Danny watched another 20 go down in flames. And now the dealer was gloating.

Danny doubled his bet. She couldn't possibly do it again.

Two more tens for Danny. A three for the dealer. Relief was on the way. This time, the dealer had a ten under. That was 13. An ace was next and next and next. With each ace, Danny became more agitated, and the dealer became more thrilled at her luck. But come on, he had 20 and now she was showing 16. If the next card was anything but a five, Danny couldn't lose. For just a second or two, time stopped.

Danny realized he was about to get her back. It was almost impossible for him to lose this hand. He stared right into her cold eyes. And she rolled over another five. 21. You lose, Danny. You lose again.

Danny pounded his hand on the table over and over again. His voice was raised: "You can't do that!" Bang, his hand smacked the table. "You can't do that to me!" He slapped the felt again. "No fucking way you can draw three straight fives to get 21 and beat all those tens!" By now, the dealer was more than nervous. She was calling the pit boss for help. And I was pulling Danny away from the table. He was out of control.

"She can't do that to me," he kept murmuring. "This can't be happening." By now, a security guy was walking over. Danny finally caught hold of himself. "No problem here, sir. We're all right. We're just enjoying this woman turning our 20s into losing hands."

Years later, we still joke about the dealer calling for help: "Lady Fatima needs help on Aisle Nine. Crazy man stamping his hands on the table!"

Danny lost his mind when the dealer beat him three times in a row. He lost control of his emotions. But he didn't lose all of his money. Just those three bets. Danny had enough resources to play again, but I insisted, and so did the casino—we had to go somewhere else to play.

What does this gambling story have to do with this Hermanism?

**It demonstrates that even if you have a winning hand, you can lose. And so you better have more money than you thought you needed.**

Most people don't think about the financial consequences of having a business fail, or at least fail to be great. They lose their savings, and they lose out on other income opportunities. They also get into debt. They feel the pain of credit card interest, with no revenue stream to help them escape.

**Before you start a new company, you should realize that it will most likely cost you more than you anticipate. It will take longer than you expect to hit the revenue stream that you have predicted. And it will cost more to do business than you planned on.**

And yet, most people start with no cushion. Most investors have no place left to draw from should they need more than they initially planned on. And therefore many companies fail simply because they can't afford to stay alive long enough to succeed.

A few years ago, my son's restaurant was named the best restaurant in Baltimore by a major food critic in the largest newspaper in town. We lost about $150,000 that year. My son didn't have that kind of money. Luckily, my wife and I were able to help him weather the storm.

The next year, the restaurant's losses were down to $50,000. Again, my son would have gone under, but we had the necessary capital to prop up the business. Then, in year three, welcome to the promised land: profits. He had made it. Because we could afford to keep him alive long enough to make it.

The restaurant remained profitable until he sold the business in the fifth year. And he made even more profit from the sale of the restaurant—because it was making money, not losing it. Had he been forced to rely strictly on his own financial resources, his story would have turned out much differently.

**Your mousetrap may be better. Your idea may be a winner. But can you sustain yourself long enough for the business to mature into profitability?**

# Hermanism #18

## THINK OF THE ARTISTS WHO HAD TO DIE TO BE SUCCESSFUL.

If you are doing something only for the money or recognition, remember that sometimes those things may be a long time coming. Artists whose works bring millions today died penniless. Innovators now praised for their genius were barely noticed or even scoffed at when they were working.

**Do not expect immediate success.** Sometimes it takes a while for the world to recognize a good thing. Take steps to make people aware of your work, your business, your service, or your product. And then have patience.

I constantly struggle with my impatience. I speak to one of my editors almost daily, and I frequently annoy her by wondering aloud why it is taking so long for the first book to become a huge success. We have never had a bad review. The cover says it will entertain, empower, and enlighten, and many who have read the book have said it does just that. So what's the problem?

One day, my book distributor said something that put my frustration into perspective: "Book sales move at the speed of a glacier."

It takes time for the reviewers to review the book. For the media to discover the book. For the early buyers to actually read the book—and then tell others about it.

The snowball starts out tiny and rolls down the hill quite slowly at first. Somewhere down the mountain, it may pick up speed and become an avalanche of success. But it takes time.

No matter how talented you are or how hard you try, realize that it will take time for the world to recognize your brilliance. In the meantime, you better be doing something that you enjoy.

# HERMANISM #19

## EXPERIENCE ALWAYS COSTS YOU SOMETHING, AND IT IS ALWAYS WORTH THE COST.

Going to school provides you with formal training in a certain subject matter. Actually doing that something provides you with experience. Read about baseball, and you have an understanding of the game. Face a ninety-mile-an-hour fastball, and that experience heightens your understanding.

It doesn't matter how small your business enterprise is or how young or old you are when you start it, the experience you gain is priceless. **Commerce is best learned by experience.** It's a basic "find a need, fill a need" game. Sell lemonade in the summer, and people will buy it up like crazy. Try selling it in the winter and people will say, "Is that Jones kid nuts?"

We all knew young kids who worked odd jobs. I shined shoes before I was five years old. That red shoe-shine kit I dragged into Sol's Tavern on Harford Road put my first earnings into my pocket. Why do I still remember that? Because it made me feel good. I provided a service, and people thanked me with money.

Of course, I was too young to get the nuances of the men laughing, stuffing their dimes through the money slot, and then watching me try to snap a cloth over the polish I put on their shoes—like a damn monkey doing parlor tricks.

All I remember is that I did some work and I earned some money. I had walked across the park, and there was something on the other side for me. (If you don't know what park I'm talking about, re-read Hermanism #1.) At that age, one dollar was like a million. I thought anything was possible if I just worked hard enough. Think it's a coincidence that I never stopped working after that?

However, experience does have a price. At sixteen, I sacrificed time with my friends to have a job washing dishes in a restaurant. No more baseball with the neighborhood kids. No more pitching quarters against the schoolhouse steps with my buddies. No more time for the girlfriend I had and loved. I gave up those things to go to work.

But I learned so much from working. To be on time. To show respect for management. To work hard so I could get my duties done during my shift. I was still a kid, but living in an adult world.

Gaining that experience was worth way more than the money I was being paid. Because, while the money didn't last long, what I learned back then has served me well for many, many years.

And the lessons continued.

Linen Laminations lost money. That was my plaque business—a costly experience. The Wax Man was a public disaster of catastrophic proportions. Lost the house. No more Caddy. Bye-bye airplane. That was knowledge I couldn't have gotten at Harvard. Wall Street experience. It ended up costing lots and lots of money. And energy. And relationships. With all that pain, the experience better be worth it. So I made damn sure I learned something.

You see, sometimes when we fail, we bury our heads in the sand. It doesn't matter if your head is buried; the bad stuff still happens. So why not take your head out of the ground and look at what has happened? Learn something from it! If a thousand of you reading this book are business owners, then five hundred of you will soon wish your head was buried in the sand. Resist! Resist, I say.

Hold your head up high. Ask a million questions of yourself and those around you. Analyze the situation. Learn from your experience. Make your failure worthwhile.

# HERMANISM #20

## LISTEN TO OTHERS WHO KNOW WHAT THEY ARE TALKING ABOUT.

Unless you are the rare person inventing a brand-new product that the world has never seen before, someone, somewhere, has already done what you plan to do with your business. And even if your product is unique, many of the steps you'll need to take will be the same as others have taken before you.

Music, books, movies, clothing design, service businesses—they have all been done before. Successfully.

If you want to make money doing something, you will need to do it better, faster, cheaper, or in a way that's somehow more appealing to customers. And the best way to learn how to do that is to watch what already successful businesses are doing. Learn from their successes and from their failures.

I am a very successful businessman. But as of yet, not such a successful author. So I hired professionals to help me with my books. And I listened to them.

Because I have done so many different things, I have a unique perspective to share with others, lessons from my experiences that only I can relate. My product is my point of view. But if I told stories that sounded like gobbledygook, no one would buy the books. And so I listen to Clarinda Harriss and Carmen Walsh, two highly skilled professionals in the writing world.

One thing about successful people that I have noticed: they don't mind sharing their knowledge with others who seem interested in learning. My son, Chef Edward Sweetman, is a genius with food. There are few chefs at his level. And yet I have seen him take time to teach even the newest beginners—as long as they demonstrate a respect for the food world and show a desire to learn.

At times, being a leader means being fearless. It means having to make decisions. It means that others can follow you. That you don't mind being in charge. **But it also means listening to and learning from others who have been there, done that.**

Whatever business venture you are considering— think about who in that field might take your call and answer your questions. Put your ego aside. Admit your ignorance. Seek them out and ask your questions.

What if you're not ready with specific questions or you just aren't comfortable asking them directly? Maybe you're still in the early stages of your idea. Read a book instead. Listen to a tape. Watch a movie. Search the Internet. Look for newspaper and magazine articles.

Manufacturing data can be found in a thousand sources. Retail information has existed since the first marketplace opened. There is an immense amount of information out there—information from people who are way ahead in the game you want to play. You would be foolish not to learn from their experiences.

People who think they know it all and don't need to listen to others to build their businesses have forgotten something: why they started their businesses in the first place. They observed what others were doing and believed that they could do it better, faster, or more profitably. They were learning from others then. They should continue on that path.

# HERMANISM #21

## KNOW MATH OR NO MONEY.

If you do not understand the number details of what you are trying to do, you probably won't enjoy a big payday. Regardless of what field you're in.

Musicians take gigs just to play a certain arena. To get exposure. Expenses be damned. Gas to travel there be damned. Overnight stays be damned. We are playing at such and such place. This can go on for months, years even. From venue to venue, they get exposure, but go backwards financially. Many of these musicians have to sell appliances or wait tables to pay off the credit card debt they run up getting exposure. And that exposure may never get them closer to the financial success they're seeking.

Musicians aren't the only ones wearing number blinders though. Retail business owners seldom understand the math of their operations. I buy something for $1 and mark it up to $2, so I make $1 of profit. Bullshit. What about including in your math the number of times your inventory turns over in a year? And how much of that $1 profit is eaten up by the costs of your rent, labor, insurance, loan interest, heat, light, power, etc.? Oh yeah. That math counts too.

The math doesn't include just the obvious numbers. Let's say your barbershop is busy all day with six chairs. Mine only has five, and they're only 80% full. You must be making more money than I am, right? Wrong. My barbers take a lower percentage cut than yours do. I own my building; you pay rent to someone else. I gross less, but make more money than you—because of the math, not because of the number of workers or customers.

**Math is key to any business success.** If you do not understand all of the math ramifications of making your products, storing your products, selling your services, renting your space, and everything else that goes into your business, the only way you will ever make real money is to be downright lucky.

You have to be willing to study the numbers. Know the numbers. And know what buttons to push to change the numbers if you want any money left over at the end of the month.

# HERMANISM #22

## KNOWING HOW HARD IT IS TO MAKE MONEY MAKES IT EASIER TO MAKE MONEY.

Unless you come from a wealthy family or you're content to live on welfare, you probably work to make money. And let's face it: work is hard.

My brother and I used to discuss what the mindset of a pyramid builder must have been. Not the guy at the top with the whip telling the workers to get that stone up the incline and into its proper space. We wanted to know what the hell was the guy pushing the stone thinking? How did he get up every morning and face another day of back-breaking work in the hot desert sun for some sliver to eat, not much to drink, and a tent in the middle of a sandstorm?

Perhaps he felt like he was accomplishing something. Even if all he was accomplishing was not feeling the sting from that whip.

Every year, someone publishes a report about the person who commutes the farthest to get to work. I believe we are now up to a man who rides in his car more than six hours a day round trip, just to show up at the pyramid site.

We travel by subways, buses, trains, planes, trucks, even by foot. Just getting to work can be work. So we turn up the iPod, hum to the music, and never give it much thought. Why? Because we know we have to work to make money to eat and to buy the iPod so we can enjoy our trip to work. Huh?

After a while of being trained by the guys with the whips at the office or the factory or the mall, many of us start to think the same thing. How can I become the guy with the whip and not the guy pushing the stone?

So we learn the whipper's business, and we start thinking we can do it better. And we would be fairer to the other stone pushers. And nicer to the people who commissioned us to build the freaking pyramid. Hell, we should start our own company.

Millions of businesses are started this way. I can do it better. Faster. Cheaper. My damn boss has no idea what he is doing. He has no idea how hard it is to be his worker and feel that whip and produce his product—just so he can vacation with Cleopatra every weekend at his stunning desert villa. I want a villa. I can't afford it on my pay, but I could on his. Damn it. I am going to start my own company.

Most of us struggle as workers for years before taking that step. We know that it ain't easy being a worker, but realize it might be even harder being the boss. He is always there when we get there in the morning. And he's still there when we leave most nights. Not pushing stones, of course. But he does seem to meet with lots of people and spend a hell of a lot of time on the telephone.

So if you want to go from being a worker to being an owner, know that as hard as you work to make your worker salary, you better be willing to work even harder.

And if you are willing and committed, then you have a shot at being the guy on top of the pyramid.

# HERMANISM #23

## THE DESIRE TO WIN OR SUCCEED
## NUMBS THE PAIN IT TAKES TO GET THERE.

What are your goals in life? Or business? And how badly do you want those things?

Want to lose weight? Sure you do. But maybe not at the expense of eating only healthy foods and exercising every day. Almost all of us could be our ideal weight—if only we were willing to pay the price. The same principle applies in business.

When I started a franchise operation that ultimately went public many years ago, I wanted to be the CEO of a major concern. I wanted to be like Ray Kroc of McDonald's. Actually I wanted to be bigger than he was. So I worked a lot of hours and slept very little. My body was often tired, and I desperately wanted to sleep, but getting the work done when it needed to be was more important than sleeping.

Look at musicians who travel hundreds of days a year and perform night after night in front of thousands of people in concert halls across the world. Traveling beats up your body. Working hard every day beats up your body. The stress of performing in front of those thousands takes a toll on your body and mind.

I have heard Elton John in concert many times over the last thirty-five years, and he still amazes his audiences. But he has admitted the pain of all his efforts. For a long time, he turned to drugs to numb that pain. After recognizing that drugs would kill him, not prolong his success, he stopped. So, what numbs his pain now? What keeps him going? It can't be the money; he could never spend what he already has. It must be, at least in part, a desire to excel and to deliver his message through his music. And so we continue to be blessed with his performances.

Not long ago I was speaking with Kenny, the partner who took over my brokerage firm. And I started to think about the past. How had I made over two thousand trips? Renting cars and visiting owners in forty-one states. Going to court to testify, perhaps a hundred times. Spending thousands of days away from home, meeting people for whatever time I could get in a given day.

I had motivation. My goal wasn't to accumulate money or power, but rather to give each of my kids opportunity beyond what I had—or at least as much as I could provide for them.

Been there, done that. My children are grown now. They all benefited from wonderful educations and have interesting adult lives underway. The forces that once drove me to be a success at all costs no longer exist.

So when Kenny recently asked me if I wanted to work on any more deals with him, I said no. My motivation, my reason for doing it was gone. Now I would feel the pain I used to be able to ignore: the pain of traveling, fighting with lawyers, banging heads with stubborn owners. After years of building the company and making a great living from it, I had changed. I was just as smart, able to perform just as well. But I had lost the drive to do that type of work.

A funny thing happened though. After four years of running a bed and breakfast where little but time was required of me, desire started to return. Not the desire to broker a deal, but the desire to do something else. After thirty-five years of continuous work after college—chasing dollars and learning about business and people—the desire to share what I had learned began to take hold of me.

And so I wrote book one, *The Innkeeper Tales*. Even before I finished writing book one, I knew there would be a book two: the one you're reading now.

This new desire—to be in front of students, business people, and anyone else who will listen—numbs the pain that, once again, I will be on an airplane heading someplace for a short meeting with someone new, for an unknown payoff.

# HERMANISM #24

## RESPECTING EMPLOYEES COSTS ZERO DOLLARS AND PAYS HUGE RETURNS.

In the 1990s, my partners and I bought a plant in California with over three hundred employees. This factory produced a plastic item with a 28% reject rate. That meant every day, more than one out of every four items manufactured was worthless. Fortunately, because the parts were plastic, we could recycle the material and not waste the cost of the supplies. But we did lose all of the labor put into making those rejected parts. Our objective was to change the plant culture—to make the workers care more and help us decrease that reject rate, and thereby improve the company's profitability.

On our first day, we assembled the workers to introduce the new management staff—and to recognize certain key employees. I asked the man and woman who had worked at the plant the longest to step forward. Both had been there more than thirty years. We gave each of them a certificate for dinner out on the town and a raise. The workers were amazed. At a gesture that cost us less than $300 and two token raises.

We then asked all of the workers to make a list: three things that would make their jobs easier to perform or make them happier at work. We explained that we didn't expect to make all of their dreams come true, but we did intend to listen and to make the changes that we could. We were showing them that we were all on the same team.

So what did they write on their lists? You'd probably guess that most of them would say they wanted more money. You'd be wrong. These were the items they listed most often:

1. To have clean bathrooms and locker room sinks that worked.

2. To have a voice, and have management listen.

3. To know what the company was doing, where it was going, and where their future was headed.

That first weekend, we had every bathroom and locker room in the factory painted. Then we had a plumber fix all of the sinks and drains, so that everything was in working order.

Next, we had each team on the factory floor choose a representative to attend a weekly management meeting. There they could raise any concerns their teams had. At those same meetings, a management representative gave the team leaders information about the big picture of the company, which they could then take back to the rest of the workers.

What did these workers need to turn a losing operation around? New equipment? More vacation time? Higher wages? No. Just some respect.

Within six weeks, the rejection rate melted from 28% down to 3%. That meant every day we were producing 25% more product, without adding a dollar to our cost. We had increased production from about 18,000 parts per day to over 24,000. It was like we were getting 6,000 parts for free. Within three months, the plant was making over $150,000 profit per month.

We turned a losing operation into a profitable one by spending less than $5,000 to paint bathrooms, fix locker rooms, and schedule weekly meetings to share information with staff. And the employees responded with dedication and hard work.

An older man named "Sam" worked as the security guard at the front gate. Sam was a company fixture. He was in his late sixties and wore what looked like an old military uniform from his home country of Belize. Sam sure was proud of his epaulets.

As I drove into the parking lot one hot morning, I saw Sam down on his hands and knees painting the curb yellow. I asked him why he was on the ground painting curbs. He said it was part of his job and he just wanted to make us happy. I told him he should stay in his air conditioned hut. Never again was he to work out in the heat, down on his knees. I said he was a valuable man, and we certainly didn't want him falling ill. He should simply stay at his guard post and that would make me happy.

I didn't make this gesture in front of anyone else. I didn't do it to prove any point. I just showed an older man respect.

Three hours later, I was walking through the plant on my morning rounds. By then the Sam story had spread like wildfire. Every worker recognized that the gesture I made for Sam was a simple show of respect. Sam was a senior man, fragile in health. Not someone who should be doing manual labor.

The workers applauded me as I walked past their stations. They were thanking me for caring about Sam, because that meant I cared about them too.

# Hermanism #25

## "Will this airplane ever fly?" If it was designed to fly, it might, despite how it looks.

According to the principles of aerodynamics, the bumble bee should not be able to fly. But we know, especially those of us who have been stung by one, that the bumble bee somehow figured out how to work around those principles and fly anyway.

In the 1940s, Howard Hughes built the Spruce Goose. This flying boat, created to transport men and materiel across the Atlantic, was made primarily of wood, as metal was scarce during the war years. (By the way, the wood was mostly birch, not spruce as the nickname implies.) Skeptics declared the gigantic craft would never fly. But it did. The Goose flew one time, for less than one mile. Hughes spent millions of dollars on it with absolutely no return on his investment. But it did fly.

For a more profitable example, let's look at FedEx. When Fred Smith proposed to build a company that could deliver documents to every doorstep in America in just one day, not many people believed he could do it. Think about it. He was going to compete with the United States Postal Service, by charging about $10 to deliver a package that the USPS would deliver for $1. Sure it would get there faster, but how important was that? And even if the customer would pay the extra $9, think about the planes, trucks, and people required—the logistical nightmare of such a company. Surely this idea couldn't fly. But today, FedEx works just like Smith envisioned it, even better probably.

A few years ago, it seemed impossible that anyone would pay $4 for a cup of coffee. Or $3 for a bottle of water at an airport shop, when a nearby drinking fountain offers it up for free. Today, those are common occurrences that we all take for granted.

Companies are succeeding every day—despite the fact that on paper they don't seem like they could ever fly. Use your imagination, and you might create something that soars.

# HERMANISM #26

## IS IT A FAILURE TO GET A SECOND DEGREE FROM THE SCHOOL OF HARD KNOCKS? GRADUATE AGAIN AND MOVE ON.

Attention all business owners: There will come a day when you will no longer own your company. Oh sure, a few owners do die at their desks. But it's statistically improbable that you will own the same business you do now in just a few short years.

So what do you do then? If your business tanks, do you give up your dreams and go to work at the nearest mall for virtually no money, no control over your schedule, and absolutely no satisfaction?

Successful people who already have lots of money continue to work for more. So it seems to me that the owner of a failed company definitely needs to try again. But what if that next venture also fails? Is it then time to give up? Lie down and die?

You've failed again. So what? No one will shoot you. And unless you committed a few crimes along the way, they won't put you in jail.

**If this is your second brush with death, remember the pain of the first one. And remember that at some point you got over it. You will move on to try yet again.**

And this time, you'll be armed with an even better education.

# HERMANISM #27

## RENT: DO YOU KNOW THE "UNIT COST" OF YOUR RENT? HOW MUCH OF EACH ITEM YOU SELL OR EACH HOUR YOU BILL DOES THE RENT COST?

If someone offers you the choice between owning a building that you will lease out to a restaurant owner or owning the restaurant business, be the landlord. Most restaurants fail in their first two years. That means in a few years if you're the restaurant owner, you'll probably be gone, and if you're the landlord, you'll still be there collecting a rent check.

Business owners seem to take rent for granted. But when you rent, the property will never be yours. You own only the business on the property. And that can be a problem, as the next story illustrates.

I once bought a gas station business. The previous owner had occupied the same spot for years. It was on a major road in Baltimore: tens of thousands of cars whizzed by daily. There were three pump islands with three pumps each—nine pumps to sell gas to the guzzling public. In the previous owner's earlier days, he had repaired cars in the two service bays. But he became tired of dealing with the public. He had the service bays scrubbed spotless, then painted to look like a little gas station museum. The lifts worked, but the only time they went up and down was to fix a few friends' cars.

So there was no auto service. No Quick Stop store, no candy or bread, no coffee. The guy just sold gas. Lots of gas. About 80,000 gallons a month of gas.

But he didn't own the land the business sat on. The land was owned by a large oil company. Which meant that he could sell only that company's brand of gas. And that he had to pay rent. When I bought the business, the rent was $400 a month.

This station was in a part of town where many of the people owned older cars. The kind that needed their mufflers replaced. So I decided to expand the gas station business and put in a muffler repair shop.

The plan worked. From the day we began installing mufflers, we were busy. We also advertised oil changes for $9.95. Not only did the bays become active, but because we had more than just gas to rely on, we could lower the gas price a tiny bit. And the lower gas price attracted more customers. Within a few months, we were selling 100,000 gallons of gas a month. And bringing in thousands of dollars each week in the service bays.

Everyone noticed the increase in business—especially the rep from the big oil company that owned the property. He would stop by the place each week and tell me what a wonderful job I was doing. He always smiled and said, "Ka-ching, Herman, ka-ching." I'm sure he thought I stayed up late just counting my money.

Not so fast. Remember, I had lowered the price of gas to increase sales, and that lowered my profit margin per gallon. Sure, we did more volume, but we stayed at about the same profit level as the previous owner. And for the new services we offered, we had to pay mechanics and buy car parts and advertise. So while we had created new revenue, it certainly was not all profit.

Ka-ching, my ass.

And it went downhill from there. In the rental agreement that I had inherited when I bought the business, there was a clause that the big oil company could adjust the rent—allowing it to control its profit level.

Mr. Big Oil Rep had run back to his offices to tell them that my location's revenue had significantly increased. Wouldn't this be a good time to let that rent escalation clause go into effect?

The company's adjusted rent offer for a new three-year lease started at $2,000 a month. That's a big jump from $400! Multiply this bullshit by thousands of gas stations across the country, and you can see why that company makes billions in profit.

I had sold 25% more of that company's product than had previously been sold—and still paid the same price for it. I certainly hadn't gotten any volume discount from the oil company. I had also paid mechanics, bought parts, and advertised repair services—none of which the oil company contributed to. And those money grubbers jacked my rent up by five times.

My business was a huge success. For them. We argued. They won.

I immediately sold the business for three times what I paid for it a year earlier—and I got the last laugh.

# HERMANISM #28

## PREPARATION. YOU CAN'T EVER SAY ENOUGH ABOUT PREPARATION.

Product manufacturers include assembly directions for a reason: to make it easier for you to put their products together. So ... do you read the directions or jump right in?

Admit it. If you always read the directions and neatly lay out all the parts before you start putting something together, I bet you are more comfortable being an employee than an owner.

Most entrepreneurs tend to think they don't need directions. I think it's about maintaining control and having a sense of adventure. Funny thing though. Eventually even the entrepreneurs end up consulting those damn directions. Then they start cussing because they skipped a step and have to go back and undo three. I've done this enough times that the frustration memory kicks in when I open a new box, and I find myself at least glancing at the directions before I start screwing pieces together.

Many failures could be avoided if entrepreneurs recognized the need for better preparation. Not just for the role they will play in owning a company, but also for the roles everyone else will play.

In football, the quarterback needs to know what every one of his teammates on the field is going to do when that ball is snapped. He also has to prepare his teammates to react to the other team. That requires speculating about what the other team's players might do and preparing for several different options.

You have to be the quarterback and make sure your business is prepared for everything. Give your employees the right equipment to do their jobs. Teach them what you want them to do, the procedures you want them to use. Give them the directions you so want to ignore. That's right. Now you have to write the damn things, not just read them.

Prepare for that upcoming presentation or meeting. Think about the audience or client. Check that the merchandise displays are attractive, that all the items are priced, that your A-V equipment is working properly. Make sure the shop is clean before you open the door.

Prepare until you can't prepare any more—or your competition may sack you.

# HERMANISM #29

## SUCCESSFUL PEOPLE HAVE THE SAME 24 HOURS IN A DAY THAT OTHERS HAVE. THEY JUST USE THE HOURS DIFFERENTLY.

There was a time I could work six or seven days a week with only about four hours of sleep a night. But getting up at 5 A.M. got old a long time ago. My passion for work had waned. That is, until the book writing started. The next thing I knew, I was waking up early again. I couldn't wait to hit the keyboard.

**If you are passionate about something, your mind may sometimes get ahead of what your body can accomplish.** After all, it may take a good idea only ten seconds to pop out of your head—and then many hours, days, weeks, months, or even years to make that idea into a reality.

When my first book came out, I wanted to send copies to all of the college department heads for Business and English. Simple. Just look up the colleges online, find the teacher lists, jot down some names, and ship off the books. Hell, even if it had been that simple, it would have taken hours.

But it wasn't that simple. Each college website was different. And on some, you couldn't access the full staff listings unless you were a registered student. So this simple idea began requiring calls to the colleges to identify the correct individuals to receive the book. Finally, a list was completed, letters were written, and the books were packed, stamped, and delivered to the post office.

I thought sending books to college professors so they could see this (in my opinion, brilliant) work and share it with their students was a great idea. And so, despite the hard work and extra hours it took, I got it done. I sent about eighty books in all, to every English department head and Business department head at every college in Maryland.

Out of those eighty, four acknowledged receiving the book. And I bet fewer than ten read it.

Let's review. I am an expert in dealing with financially troubled businesses. I've consulted with more than a thousand companies all over America. There was now a book available about many of those ventures. And I had offered to come to the colleges and speak to the students, to impart some real-life wisdom, at no charge.

Surely this would solicit a response?

The silence was deafening. But by the time you are reading this, I will have spoken to many students at those colleges. Because I still believed in my idea.

You may be wondering what this has to do with the Hermanism about everyone having the same 24 hours a day.

Well, since I believed in my idea of spreading my message to college students, and since one way I had spent time attempting to realize that idea hadn't worked yet, then I had two choices: (1) give up on my goal or (2) spend more time on it, perhaps taking a different approach.

At this point, many people quit. Faced with rejection, or even the lack of acceptance, they retreat.

My partner, Kenny, believes that people do one of two things when faced with a choice. They either do something to seek pleasure or do nothing to avoid pain. It would be a pleasure to see college students and interact with them at this point in my career. It was a little painful to have so many teachers not respond at all. Doing nothing would avoid any more of that pain. But doing something might gain me the pleasure I was seeking.

And doing something means working. Working to come up with a new idea. Spending time executing that idea. And that means giving up hours in the day that could be spent on other pursuits.

You have to decide what effort you are willing to make. You must choose how much time you will spend trying to be successful.

Usually the people who are at the forefront of an idea or business are willing to put their all into it to make it successful. But at times their efforts are severely hampered by those around them, those who do not share their vision or their passion.

When you are choosing what time you are willing to spend on your venture, you must consider the impact of that decision. Are you willing to miss out on family dinners, your kids' ballgames, playing poker with the boys, or even just sitting on your ass reading a good book?

Finding the extra hours in a day you will need is easy if you do not care what happens to your life. But knowing that your life interacts with your family and friends will sometimes eat away at your drive to succeed.

Being an entrepreneur isn't any harder than playing the piano or selling insurance or teaching school. Every vocation has its own demands. But being an entrepreneur may entail more financial risk. More headaches as an owner. But first and foremost, more of your time.

I have experienced a divorce, with someone I loved dearly. Clearly one of the causes of my divorce was my incredible drive to succeed not matching up with my wife's view on how our time should be spent. Looking back, I am sure I should have done a better job of communicating what was going on inside my head. Why it was so important to spend my time doing what I was—for the good of the entire family, versus what surely seemed like a selfish need to accomplish my goals.

**To succeed, you have to make the others around you understand that what you are doing is as important to you as the air you breathe. And so to be a happy person, you have to put in that time.**

# HERMANISM #30

## DON'T EXPECT TO BE ABLE TO RUN A MARATHON IF YOU WORK OUT BY ONLY WALKING A BLOCK.

To give your business a fighting chance to succeed, you have to build into your business plan enough time—and the resources to survive that time.

If your cash flow won't start to cover your expenses until your sixth month in business, then you can't start with four months' cash. Regardless of how hard you may pray, you will run out of capital before you have a chance to succeed.

You have to be able to work longer than you expected and have the mental, physical, and capital reserves to go far enough to win. And that means you can't save just a few bucks and get started. Or half think out the plan and still win.

**Business always adheres to certain principles. One of those is that business doesn't pay any attention to your desires; it answers only to the elements of action and resources.**

If you think you can drive five hundred miles on a single gallon of gas, you are ignoring the principles of gas mileage (at least with today's technology).

And when you run out of gas before you reach your destination, it won't be because you didn't want to get there badly enough. It will be because you didn't plan and prepare properly for the long run.

HERMANISM #31

## IF IT WERE EASY,
## EVERYBODY WOULD BE DOING IT.

This phrase was spouted to me by one of my favorite bankers over and over again.

It doesn't require much explanation. But it is a handy phrase to remember when things get tough. Because there will undoubtedly be times when you will ask yourself why it has to be so damn hard.

That's when you remind yourself why you are doing what you're doing, what you hope to achieve, what the reward may be.

You're not doing it because it's the easy thing to do.

# HERMANISM #32

## EXPECTING TOO MUCH FROM OTHERS IS TOO MUCH FOR YOU TO EXPECT.

Many employees are equally as skilled as their bosses. Their position is not a question of talent. They just don't want to live, breathe, and eat the stuff. On the other hand, entrepreneurs are driven; they often focus so much on their business goals that they ignore other aspects of life. Bad entrepreneurs are the ones who don't recognize that distinction.

As an entrepreneur, you must remember that while you want to spend extra hours at your desk working on an important project, others may not want to give up their evenings at home with the family or their weekend plans. Their commitment level is not the same as yours.

Even within a nine-to-five workday, the difference is obvious. You are in the middle of a project. Lunch goes by and you don't care. Hell, you don't even notice. So when you call a colleague with a question and you're told he went to lunch, you get irked. What do you mean he's at lunch? We have work to do.

One Friday, I was working with my publicist and another member of my team on the marketing campaign for my first book. We were collaborating by phone and e-mail on a press release that was to be sent out "right away." After we had gone through several drafts, each of us was finally satisfied. I asked the publicist to circulate the final version, as I wanted to send it along with some books later that day.

It was twenty minutes after noon in the publicist's time zone. She e-mailed me this reply: "Our offices close at noon on Fridays, so I will send you the final copy first thing Monday morning."

She didn't hear me gasp when I read her message. Before I burst a vein, I reminded myself that everyone else in the world does not work on the same schedule as I do. And I can't expect them to.

The people I shipped the books to later that day didn't get a copy of that press release. And I lived to see another day.

# HERMANISM #33

## FAILURE ISN'T FATAL.

The note on my apartment door said I had just seven days to vacate or all my belongings would be put in the parking lot. Another reminder of my failure.

My airplane was gone by then, and the fancy cars. My wife's house had been sold so she would have money to take care of the kids. At the office, the IRS was looking for someone to talk to. Shareholders were wondering what had happened to all the money they had invested. There were months of uncashed paychecks in my drawer because the company didn't have the money to cover them.

My business had gone, in just three years, from a small startup to a booming enterprise. From working out of a single station detailing cars for five dealerships to being licensed to franchise in thirty-five states and providing products and services to over three hundred dealerships. We were headline news; magazine articles were written about us. I had taken the company public and cheered with the stockholders when I saw the stock selling for twenty times the initial price.

And now the stock was wallpaper. Poof. It was all gone. And I was broke.

**I had lost money, possessions, prestige, lots of time, and the respect of many people. Total failure.**

I couldn't figure it out. We had a great product and a great concept put together by talented people who worked tirelessly to make the company succeed. Was it my poor leadership that took us down? Was it my fault?

It had to be my fault. Someone had to be blamed for this disaster. Good ideas do not just fail. Surely some of my decisions in the last three years should have been different. But they weren't. It was over.

I felt terrible for everyone's losses. But one thing stuck with me through the weeks following the downfall. I truly believed that I had done the best I could. There was nothing else I could have done to make it work. And I had sacrificed all I had trying, whether others believed it or not.

**So, I could either wallow in the failure or get up and start again.**

I wasn't dead. The failure hadn't killed me. Even though the pain of losing was incredible, I was still breathing. I hadn't suffered a potentially terminal illness. I had just tried at a business and failed.

No one sent in armed troops to shoot me because I had lost other people's money. No one held me down and tortured me. Even the IRS gave me a few years to clean up what was owed.

So, five days after a catastrophic failure, I simply started doing something else. And that something else developed into my most successful endeavor ever, success on a national scale.

# HERMANISM #34

## IS IT BETTER TO SQUEEZE A HIGHER PRICE, OR CHARGE LESS AND CALCULATE THE DIFFERENCE AS PAYMENT FOR A NEW "AMBASSADOR" WHO WILL RAVE ABOUT THE VALUE HE GOT FOR HIS MONEY?

Pricing in any business is very sensitive. Look for volume and price low, and the margin leaves little room for error. Price high because there is no real competition, and you drive business away.

Let's look at hotel rooms as an example. If your hotel is next to the city's downtown tourist haven, within walking distance of two major sports stadiums, then you can charge whatever the demand allows. That might be over $200 per night. And you can charge even more for parking and meals.

If someone is coming to town for a convention that's taking place right next door to your hotel, then your hotel is the most logical choice, right? It's the most convenient. But most people will still look for a better price elsewhere and determine whether that convenience is worth the money.

The bed and breakfast I've been running for several years is one mile from those city hotspots. That's one mile of inconvenience. But there is a Light Rail system that can transport people to those places in under five minutes. Convenience problem solved. So let's talk about some less obvious factors.

## Upgrades and Repeat Business

Large hotels don't distinguish between single travelers and couples very well. Almost all hotel rooms are doubles, for economy reasons. And yet almost half of all convention-goers travel alone. Or with a work colleague, someone they'd rather not share a room with.

At our B&B, we have a few single rooms. They're small, with a twin bed and a small bathroom (shower, no tub). And we rent them for $88 a night, not $200. So those two colleagues could afford to pay for separate rooms. Awkwardness avoided.

Last year, over 1,200 solo travelers rented a single room with us. But we have only three single rooms. If we rented all three 365 nights of the year, that would be 1,095 total. How did we rent more singles than we had?

We upgraded many of those solo travelers to double rooms with beautiful queen beds. And we gave them parking and served them breakfast at no additional charge. While the guests staying in the singles had smaller rooms than they would have at a large hotel, they still enjoyed the same beautiful linens, cable TV, and other amenities.

We have been upgrading guests in this way for almost five years. If you call and rent a standard room for $115, and on that day a mini-suite is open (which normally rents for $155), you may find yourself sleeping in the best room at the place.

And while travel across the country decreased and other B&Bs suffered from declining occupancy rates, we grew 7% each year. Why is that?

The guests we upgrade feel great as soon as they check in and find out they are being given a better room, at the same price. They become spokespersons for the place. And often, those single business travelers who end up in larger rooms fall in love with something about the city and bring their spouses back later to show them around.

Where do you think they stay when they come back? That's right. The place where they got the free upgrade.

Our repeat business has overcome any decline in the overall number of travelers.

## Service and Referral Business

All employees working on commission know how tricky it can be. They know that the company hiring them for their service is trying to save money. And so many try to get the highest possible commission for each job.

I believe this is the wrong approach.

I believe that almost all of us work primarily for the money. (If they took away your paycheck, would you show up tomorrow?) But I also believe you should never chase a commission.

When you sell a product or service for a commission, you need to remember something. Each day, you will need new customers. Sell one customer and he's gone; you're out searching for another one.

**My philosophy has always been to get my last customer to help me find my next customer.** For you to make that happen, the last customer has to feel great about your service and your price. Getting gouged is not something he wants revealed. So if you "got him" in the last deal, then he will not say a word to others about using your service. You're on your own to find your next customer.

Instead of trying to negotiate a higher commission, you need to concentrate on providing the best service possible, giving the best effort possible, and making the best deal possible for that customer. **And while you are cashing the commission check, that customer will be selling you to your next customer.**

At my brokerage firm, we had a set fee schedule. We determined the usual expenses for handling the sale of a company. And we didn't negotiate our fee or expenses with our clients. We concentrated on getting the companies sold quickly and for the highest dollar amount possible.

At times, we exceeded our expense budget, but we never charged the client for the excess. We let the client know that we were over budget—either for more trips needed than expected, more marketing or advertising expenses than normal, or simply more postage because more people were looking at the deal. Sometimes more than the normal number of court appearances was required. But I viewed all of that as part of our service.

And so, on occasion, our fee wasn't all profit. Sometimes we were underwater on the expenses and had to trim that amount off the top before splitting the commission among the staff. But we never asked a client to pay more.

**My philosophy was to do deals—as many deals as possible—and the money would take care of itself.**

Perhaps we could have made one or two percent more from a deal here or there because the clients were willing to pay more, but so what. Over the course of twenty years, we received calls about new deals from hundreds of bankers and lawyers who knew, and respected, the way we did business.

They were ambassadors for our company. They never stopped telling their clients about our service. About how many hours we put in on a deal. How fair we were with prospects trying to buy a company. How honest we were in speaking for the best deal for the company, not the one that got us the highest commission.

Ask any broker how much he values a referral deal and you will understand that you should never chase money.

Chase deals instead. The money will follow.

# HERMANISM #35

## IBM SAID IT BEST ... THINK.

I used to love when I had to spend hours on a plane and then drive another couple of hours to get to a meeting. Because that was "free" time. Time for me to think. Time to go over the things we would discuss at the meeting, the issues the lawyers or bankers or owners may raise. And I'd prepare answers for those challenges. If I owned the business I was visiting, I would go over the reports that the president had given me. And I'd be ready for the chief financial officer when I arrived.

I first learned of this concept in flight school. Early on in my training, I was always nervous on a ride. And I'd get too sick to land the plane. A friendly colonel gave me a solution. "Fly the ride," he said. "Go over in your mind what you are going to do up there, and then when you do it, you will feel less out of control and less nervous."

He taught me to sit in a chair and imagine each phase of the flight, while I was safely on the ground. Take off, turn out of traffic, fly to your practice site, do your maneuvers, fly back to the base, and land.

It worked. The next time I went up in the air, I was able to complete the flight without getting sick.

The long flights and drives that my partners complained about allowed me time to "fly the ride" for my meetings. I practiced every step in my head. Thought it out. And so when I got to my destination, I was ready for anything.

**Take advantage of every moment you can. Think. Prepare for every possibility you can imagine, for whatever someone may throw at you. Fly the ride.**

## HERMANISM #36

### KNOW YOUR OWN LIMITS OR YOUR SUCCESS WILL BE LIMITED.

I have enjoyed many successes in my life. But I couldn't have achieved any of them without the help of other people—people who could do something that I couldn't do myself.

I approach every project I take on with this thought in mind: I may be the one in charge, but I do not know everything.

For example, my books. I am a business failure expert, not a computer expert. So when it came to creating actual books from my raw manuscripts in Microsoft Word, I didn't have a clue. I needed help, and I found it.

The cover of my first book is beautiful. So is Carmen Walsh, the lady who designed it. Sure, I gave her input on what I wanted, but she took my amateur point of view, implemented it, and then added immense value with her skills. My limits had been reached, and she took me further. Same thing on this book cover. I love it. It started with my idea that business is about time and money. She conveyed that idea in a manner that makes people pick up the book to look inside. You did, right?

And you have read enough pages by now to be thankful that I have a team of great editors. Clarinda Harris is a genius. She knows how to take my words and make them communicate better. And that is why she's on my team. Because she has skills that are beyond my limits. This book and the one before it would never have seen the light of day without her professional help. The same goes for Carmen Walsh, who acted as the main editor on this book. She works tirelessly to help me get my message out in a way that is easy to understand, and it still sounds like I'm the one doing the talking.

Any success these books achieve will not be the result of my knowledge or my storytelling. Any success will be the result of the combined skill sets of all of the people involved with the books. I will succeed only because I recognized that I needed people with talents I don't possess myself.

Of course, working with others can present its own set of challenges, as you read in Hermanism #32.

Some people will tell you that I am hardheaded. Stubborn. Obstinate. A control freak of legendary proportions. But the dishwasher at our restaurant will also tell you that I talk to him and listen to him. The twenty-two-year-old innkeeper at our B&B will acknowledge that she can tell me I am wrong without fear of her head being cut off.

Some who have seen "the Herman wrath" say that I am nuts. I want perfection. I demand impossible things from others. In reality, what I want is maximum effort, not necessarily perfect results.

And, at the end of the day, regardless of who I involve in a project and ask to make decisions, I am the one responsible for those decisions. Asking for help from others who can add value to your project does not mean you are abdicating power. Power is something you take, not something you are given.

Take the power over your project by realizing your limits. Seek advice and help wherever you can. If you don't recognize your limits and recruit others to help you exceed those limits, your success will never reach its full potential.

# HERMANISM #37

## IT WAS ONLY FAILURE IF YOU FAILED TO LEARN; OTHERWISE, IT WAS EXPERIENCE.

Money is a goal. But it is not the only goal. Winning is a goal. But not everyone can win every time.

So why do we play the game? We play to get better. Start a new sport. Golf, for instance. If you don't shoot par your first day, do you give up? No, because you want to challenge yourself to get better. And because we also play just to play, to enjoy the game itself.

Owning a business is like playing golf. It's about more than making money. It's about wanting to be in control. About having the power to make decisions. About doing what you enjoy. If you don't make money at a business venture, that doesn't mean it's a complete failure.

Every business effort you make offers valuable lessons. If you aren't continually learning, then you aren't paying attention.

Even our earliest attempts at business can teach us a lot. Consider Harriet's first foray into commerce:

Seven-year-old Harriet has a lemonade stand in her front yard. Mom gives her the lemonade, the cups, and the ice. Harriet gets all the money—100% profit. The next day, Mom takes out fifty cents for the lemonade powder she used. Harriet just learned the cost of goods sold lesson. That it takes money to make money.

Harriet spends four straight afternoons at her stand and sells several glasses of lemonade each day. She misses playing hopscotch with her friends though, so she quits the lemonade business. In those four days, she learned about customer service, pricing goods, even making change for a dollar. She also learned that having a business requires sacrifice. Was her lemonade stand a failure?

My plaque business failed. The gas station I owned had to be sold because the oil company raised the rent. The automotive products company I took public crashed. But those "failures" gave me knowledge I could use in working with financially troubled companies. And in the next twenty years, my brokerage firm made millions in fees.

That level of success would not have been possible without the knowledge I gained from my earlier ventures. So, no, I don't consider those early deals failures. They were painful but valuable learning experiences, which eventually led to success.

# HERMANISM #38

## FACING REALITY IS SOBERING.
## IGNORING REALITY IS LIKE BEING DRUNK.

**Somewhere between total success and abject failure is where we live most of our lives.**

At the extremes, it's usually easy to know what to do. Your team just won the World Series. You go celebrate. You just lost every dime you own and are being evicted. You take action to survive or face even greater failure. These are situations with fairly obvious choices.

But when you are somewhere in between, exactly where are you? Which direction are you moving— closer to success or closer to failure?

To answer these questions, I relentlessly study the numbers of my business. I treat numbers as messages from the "business god." They dictate how I should proceed. If I follow the numbers, they will lead me to business heaven. If I ignore the numbers ... well, you get the idea.

To put it another way, I believe that ignoring your business numbers is like driving drunk. You may make it home safely, but it will just be dumb luck. Some people who frequently drive drunk brag that they have never had an accident. Yet. Eventually they will crash—and when they do, they may hurt themselves and/or someone else. By ignoring the reality of what they are doing, they are endangering themselves and others too.

If you ignore the reality of your business, if you don't want to be bothered with the details, then you are putting your business, yourself, and your staff in danger.

Learn the numbers. Know your staff. Have daily and weekly and yearly goals. Gain confidence from working the details of your plan. You will see the road ahead more clearly, and you'll be able to react intelligently when obstacles block your path.

Yes, sometimes facing exactly where your company is and what it needs to do to improve its situation can be quite sobering. The news is not always good. But trying to achieve success without facing the real issues is never the answer.

If you're in your neighborhood bar and you've had a few too many, who do you ask for a ride home? The guy you met a few weeks ago who's been drinking Coke all night or your best friend who's falling off his stool after too many bourbons? Think about it.

# HERMANISM #39

## EGO VERSUS INCOME: TOO MUCH EGO MIGHT EQUAL TOO LITTLE INCOME.

Being afraid to admit you are wrong can cost you more than just your pride. It can cost you money. Real big money.

One day, I was sitting in a CEO's office. Also with us was the lawyer for the bank that had loaned the CEO the money to buy the business. The CEO hadn't been making his payments to the bank. And there was not enough cash flow to pay all of the creditors, so the bank was upside down on its loan. Not good.

The lawyer, in a pleasant tone, calmly explained how the bank realized that the CEO had tried his best and that sometimes things fail. Perhaps the CEO would agree to relinquish control and let my brokerage firm sell the business and pay off what they could of the debt.

The CEO asked me what would happen to him if he agreed to let my company handle the sale. I said that if the new owners felt he added value, they may want him to stay. Otherwise, he would be gone, but the workforce would remain in place and the new owners would carry on the business. I also pointed out that since a sale wouldn't realize full payment of all the debt, the equity holders (current owners) would probably get nothing.

At that point, the lawyer spoke up again and suggested that if the CEO cooperated with this plan—which would probably return more money than any other plan—then perhaps the CEO could keep the house he had used as a loan guarantee, and his car, and continue to receive his paycheck through the conclusion of a sale. Otherwise, the bank would foreclose, take the company over, and move against the assets the CEO had pledged as a personal guarantee.

This is where ego almost cost the CEO a lot of money. More than he should have lost.

The CEO thanked us for this wonderful pitch about a plan that would demolish his life and asked us to leave.

The lawyer then asked to speak to the man's wife— for she too had signed a personal guarantee on the loan. "What would you say?" asked the CEO. "Well," said the attorney, "I would ask her to come pick you up because we are seizing the Porsche you have leased through the company. We don't need that anymore. And I would ask her where she wants to live, because we are going to foreclose on her house. And I am going to tell her that we were willing to let her keep those things and continue your paychecks, but that her husband wants to fight us—and perhaps she can talk some sense into you."

The lawyer and I were then escorted out of the building, with the agreement to meet again the next morning. It would be a showdown between the bank's lawyer and the CEO—who promptly went home and discussed his options with his wife.

At 10 A.M. the next day, the CEO handed the company keys to the bank's lawyer and walked out. And then he drove the Porsche the bank had agreed to let him keep back to his wife waiting in the house that the bank had promised not to foreclose on.

Examples like this abound. Do you hold onto a company past the point of common sense because you can't face the guys at the country club and tell them you lost your ass? Do you keep working a business that sucks your family dry because admitting to the neighbors it failed is too hard?

Look at the numbers. Take care of your family. When something is over, you can seldom bring it back to life. Shut the doors, let your ego heal, and cause as little financial damage as you can.

# HERMANISM #40

## WOULD YOU RATHER RUSH OR BE RIGHT?

Perhaps the most common character flaw in entrepreneurs is a lack of patience. We hate to wait. We may spend months thinking about doing something and then when we finally do it, we're shocked that the world does not beat a path to our door within seconds.

My first book, *The Innkeeper Tales,* came off the truck from the printers on November 10. On November 11, I wanted to know how many bookstores had copies. I quickly learned that it doesn't work that way. Seems that your book has to be submitted to the bookstores' main offices somewhere and reviewed by their staff—so that someone you've never talked to, who doesn't know a darn thing about your book, can decide whether it's worth any shelf space.

As a businessman, I understood that approximately 150,000 books are published each year and that even a large bookstore might have only 30,000 titles in stock at one time. But on the second day of my book being out in the world, I wanted to know why mine wasn't one of them.

**Patience: something that bullheaded, cockeyed optimist, thrill-seeking go-getters seldom have.**

But if you want to succeed, you must understand that all of the world does not work at the same speed as you. If you want to avoid the stress-related heart attack that can be caused by waiting for others, you'd better learn some patience. This, coming from a man who at thirty-five was told by his doctor to slow down or die young.

If we could just walk into a drugstore and buy a bottle of patience, it would solve a lot of issues for us business folk. Unfortunately we can't. So we've got to discipline ourselves. While I don't think you can simply will yourself to have more patience, I do believe you can demonstrate to yourself the need to have more patience.

Take, for instance, my Daytona Migi experience. This replicar looked like a 1954 MG-TD in every detail. When I saw its picture in *Golf* magazine, I knew it was what I wanted to drive.

That little roadster was awesome. And my Buick Riviera was nearing its final resting place. I couldn't afford much in the way of snazzy transportation to replace it, but I didn't want a Plain Jane car. How could I keep the cost down and still get a unique look? My goal was cheap but expensive-looking. Low bucks with great looks.

So I ordered the Migi instruction manual. For less than $5,000, I could buy the parts and an old Volkswagen and build the car myself. At the time, five grand didn't buy even the blandest models that carmakers were building. This little baby screamed, "Look at me and my cool ride."

I must have skipped over that last part about building it myself. Hell, I had never built a car before. And if you read my last book, you already know the many details of this saga. Here I just want to emphasize the patience-building that car experience prompted.

Day one was deciding to get the Migi. Getting from day one to actually driving the car took a lot of steps, more than I had anticipated. There were manuals to read. Parts to unpack. Components to assemble. This process would take weeks. No, months.

And I had to do something every day to reach my goal. There were fenders to put together. Seats to build. An old VW Bug to dismantle. Lots of wiring to run through tiny places.

Details, a thousand little details.

Patience.

But slowly, where there had been a pile of parts on the floor, a car was starting to appear. I could see the progress. I knew that someday soon I'd have a finished car. I just needed to have a little more patience.

Eventually, I had a beautiful car that got me around town in style. And I enjoyed driving it for several years, until the day I sold it.

Whatever stage your business is in now—whether it's just an idea in your head, or a fledgling startup, or a mature full-blown entity—you can ease your stress level by stepping back once in a while and reminding yourself to be patient.

Sometimes what you want just won't come any faster, no matter how much you want it to.

# HERMANISM #41

## MANY ENTERPRISES ARE DOOMED FROM THE BEGINNING, YET NO ONE PLANS FOR FAILURE.

I know of a new restaurant that is doomed to fail.

The five previous owners failed, every one of them. Each one spiffed up the place—with some fresh paint, newly covered chairs, or different lighting —to show the guests it was a new incarnation. And of course, each one changed the menu. If the last restaurant had failed, surely it must have been because people didn't like the menu, right?

And yet, despite the losing record, new owners keep stepping up to the plate and trying their luck. So why do I say this new owner is doomed? Because history repeats itself. Because people don't pay attention to why something has failed and they repeat the same mistakes. Menu and upholstery choices were never the problem with this restaurant.

This restaurant fails because customers come only on symphony nights. There are eighty or so dates a year when the symphony center is full and the 1,500 concert-goers need a place to eat. That has been the case for the past twenty-five years. You can put the best restaurant in the city in that spot and customers will still support the place primarily on symphony nights. How can I be so sure? Because our restaurant was named the Best Restaurant in the City and even we aren't busy on non-symphony nights. (With the regular exceptions, of course: Mother's Day, Valentine's, New Year's.)

Then how does our restaurant survive, and even make money, while virtually everyone else in the neighborhood has gone under? Because we have more than the restaurant. We have a bed and breakfast above the restaurant that produces the cash flow needed to sustain the whole operation. The rest of the restaurants in the neighborhood have nothing else to rely on. And they continually open and close. In fact, two of them have changed hands three times in the last five years.

Each time, the new operator gets a false sense of success as the concert season hits full force. Three times a week, the place is packed. He is making money on those three days. A nice profit with a room full of happy diners saying how much they love the food.

But soon he's left wondering: Where are those happy diners the rest of the year?

Many of the concert-goers are season ticket holders. They may attend ten or more concerts a year. Ten times they grace your dining room, shake your hand, and compliment your food. They may like your place so much they also come on a special occasion, like a birthday or an anniversary. That means fourteen or fifteen times a year they visit you, in your highly acclaimed fine dining restaurant.

Think for a minute. How many times a year do you eat at a nice restaurant? Not a McDonald's, mind you, but a place where the meal will cost about $50 per person. At those prices, I bet you don't go even to your favorite restaurant fifteen times a year.

Then add the drive. Nothing is near this restaurant except the concert hall. The baseball and football stadiums are a mile away. There are no movie theaters nearby. No shopping centers. The restaurant is not across the street from where you work, or even close to it. It's in the city, and you live in the suburbs.

It doesn't have a parking lot. None of the city restaurants do. You have to pay to keep your car on a lot. Or use the valet they provide—and tip the guy, so even free valet isn't free.

And then there's one more important ingredient for failure that I need to mention.

The new owner makes the mountain even higher by spending money, perhaps a few hundred thousand dollars, sprucing up the place (even if it's completely unnecessary). New art on the walls. Hell, new walls. A new bar. New lighting. New dishes. New designer glassware. New beautiful expensive stuff.

He now has a place that will continue to be sold out on the same nights the previous owner was sold out. The guests will be amazed at the beauty of his new fountains and chandeliers. And his chef will serve great food, just like the previous chef did. And the chef before that. But the owner has changed one thing that will almost certainly doom him to failure: he has created a higher cost structure for himself right from the start. He has to pay for those renovations somehow.

Nothing in this restaurant's history indicates that anyone cares about how it looks. The people came every symphony night, regardless of the atmosphere, regardless even of the menu. Pizza, burgers, or foie gras—it didn't matter. They didn't come for the food. Or the price. They came because they needed a place to eat and the other restaurants near the symphony center were sold out.

Over the last five years, not one of the new owners ever came into our restaurant and asked questions about the area—before sinking a fortune into a new restaurant. And to my knowledge, not one ever came into our place on one of those off nights and saw the empty seats in the "Best Restaurant in the City." They saw the booming concert season and leaped without another look.

No parking lot was added. No shopping mall was built nearby. A new office complex didn't spring up down the block. Nothing external to the restaurant changed. And so the new owners are doomed to repeat history. Another failed restaurant.

**Are you about to buy a business that failed, or at least struggled, under the previous ownership? If so, ask yourself some serious questions. Why will things improve just because you will be in charge? Can you change the operating cost structure? In many cases, you will actually raise the cost structure with the debt you incur to buy the business.**

What external changes have occurred that make you think business will improve? Are you bringing a customer base the current guy doesn't have? If he was profitable, why did he give it up? If his reasons are the time consumed by the business or the cash flow needs not being met, what are you going to be able to do to change those factors?

Before you leap, you need to run figures on your
cost of doing business—as it relates to the purchase
price, higher standards of operating, additional
marketing, and so on. Some cost is always higher
for the new guy versus the old guy. And, remember,
the old guy failed.

The exception is when you are able to buy a failed
business at far less than the prior owner's cost
or debt. Say you are able to buy a million-dollar
business for a few hundred thousand. Since your
cost structure is lower, you may just have a shot at
succeeding where he failed.

Unless you are able to reduce the cost structure or
some external forces have changed in your favor,
you are doomed to fail. And I would bet against
you every time.

HERMANISM #42

---

## THE TRUTH IS,
## EVEN IF YOU HAVE NOTHING,
## YOU STILL HAVE SOMETHING TO LOSE.

---

Opportunity. It is everywhere. Millions of ideas are being hatched. Maybe ten thousand new thoughts today, and ten thousand more tomorrow.

And every day, people take those new ideas and start companies on shoestring budgets. They scratch together some startup money and then spend every minute of every day trying to be successful. They think that since they started with nothing, they have nothing to lose. They'd be wrong.

You always have something to lose. Even if you have no money invested in a business, you are investing something equally as precious: your time.

We are all on the same playing field when it comes to time. Everyone gets the same amount: 365 days a year, seven days a week, twenty-four hours a day. No one gets any more than anyone else.

When you work at launching a new business, your energy is sapped—by something that has little chance of surviving. And you may very well spend all of your energy concentrating on a loser when you could have been hatching a golden egg doing something else.

If you're spinning wheels, trying to think your way out of a hole that you should never have climbed into, then you should realize something. **Your current venture might be causing you to lose out on the next opportunity.**

**There is unlimited opportunity, but limited time.** So make sure an opportunity is the best possible one for you—before you invest anything of yourself in it. Because even if it doesn't cost you any money, it surely will cost you time.

# HERMANISM #43

## WHAT IF NOBODY EVER STUCK THEIR NECK OUT AND TRIED?

Young children are fearless. They will try anything because they don't know they can get hurt. After they experience pain, some don't rush to try as many new things. They've learned to fear what could happen. But some realize the pain was often worth it. So instead of retreating, they learn to love the thrill of pushing the envelope.

**If you want a life of comfort and safety, free from pain, then don't buy or start a business. You will be hurt, damaged, made to look foolish and feel stupid. You will make your friends and family mad and suffer an immense loss of freedom. You could go broke—or worse than broke, you could lose everything and still owe money.**

It's risky making any kind of progress. Today, we take flying for granted, but a lot of test pilots died to make that a reality. If no one took chances—to start new companies, open new stores, build new technology—we wouldn't make any progress.

We wouldn't have innovations to make our lives easier, better, more exciting ...

When I was young, we had three television networks. Three choices of what to watch. For free. That was plenty: we couldn't watch more than one thing at a time anyway. We just turned on the TV set and had free entertainment. It was wonderful.

In the early 1970s, my insurance man stopped by to tell me about an investment he thought I should consider. A local doctor had decided to put a wire from house to house to hook up "cable television" in the county. It would cost each house about $10 a month to get hooked up to watch the cable TV. Huh? And I could buy stock in the new cable company for about five cents a share. Are you crazy? Who in the hell is going to spend $10 a month to watch TV when he watches for free now?

Thirty years later ... My cable bill last month was about $100—for over a hundred channels, including my old faithful three networks. It ain't free anymore.

Of course, I could pull the plug on cable and go back to the three freebies, but I don't. And neither do you. The world has moved on.

The stock I turned down was one that would have made me a millionaire many times over if I had only invested a few thousand dollars. But I didn't want to risk my money on something new, something that might fail. My loss. Someone else's gain. **On that one, I didn't stick my neck out.**

# HERMANISM #44

## LISTEN.
## SOMETIMES YOU JUST NEED TO LISTEN.

Listen to your customer. If you let your customer tell you what he wants, it's that much easier to make the sale.

In one deal I was working on, a failing company owed about $20 million in debt. Two-thirds of that debt was owed to one bank. It appeared the sale of the company would net far less than the bank was owed, so the banker was decidedly prejudiced for things to go a certain way.

In this kind of situation, at the end of the day when the bids are all in, everyone realizes that only the bank will be paid. So it is the bank and only the bank who can object to the deal—and kill our chance of completing the transaction and getting paid our fee. Which means the banker is the central player.

In a bankruptcy case, a court order spells out the details about what can transpire during the process. The order in this particular case would determine the bidding procedures. And the amounts of what would be required to post a higher bid—the increments of bidding. For example, should the bids be raised by $10,000 or by $100,000?

The banker made it clear that he didn't want to leave a penny on the table in this deal. He wanted the smallest increment possible to be in the court order.

But when my partner and I were back in our office, putting together the documents, my partner kept arguing that the current trend was to use larger increments. He wasn't listening to his customer, the banker. Was he right to argue? What would it matter how the increments were set?

Let me explain.

Let's say the increments are set at $100,000. And you, as bidder #1, bid $10 million to buy the company. Bidder #2 then bids $10.1 million. To stay in the game, you have to come back with at least $10.2 million. So whenever anyone else plays, it costs you $200,000 more. That's a substantial amount of money. And so the larger increment may force the players to drop out, ending the bidding war earlier.

On the other hand, suppose the increments are set lower, like at $10,000. The bidding might take longer because each step raises the bid only a small percentage of the price—so more bidders might be likely to increase their bids. After all, ten grand isn't much on a deal already worth ten million. But even if the bidding takes a little longer, it could be worth it.

Let's say the bidding stops at $10,190,000. If the increment had been set at $100,000 instead of $10,000, there may not have been any more bidding past $10.1 million. So, for a few extra minutes, the bank made another $90,000.

What was at stake for us? The more money bid, the higher our fee.

So not only was my partner not giving the banker something the banker specifically said he wanted; he was missing the point that we could actually make more money by doing so. My partner was more interested in showing that he was in tune with the current trends than in completing the best deal possible.

**Listen. Listen to what your customer wants.**

Stop worrying about whatever your other motivations may be. Listen carefully. Then think about all of the ramifications. And if giving your customer what he really wants costs you nothing, be quiet and make the sale.

# Hermanism #45

## IF YOU FALL DOWN, GET BACK UP.

Life is a series of ups and downs. So is business. Every day cannot be better than the one before. Bad things will happen, and you will have to recover.

Even the best cyclists in the world have crews with first aid materials ready in case of a fall. Football teams have trainers on the sidelines, equipped with stretchers, pain sprays, bandages, and oxygen to treat the players who will inevitably get hurt.

**Regardless of how good they are at what they do, successful people do not win every time they try.**

Owning a company involves thousands of decisions. Complicated financial data. A workforce that needs training, disciplining, comforting, cheering. Advertising costs without a guaranteed return on investment. Some of these things will fail. In fact, many may fail at the same time.

But if you understand the math of your business, and the math says that you are still on the right track, when these things fail, you shouldn't quit. You should get up and keep on going.

If you fall off your bike and scrape your ankle, what will make you feel better? Getting treatment and sitting out the rest of the race because it didn't go perfectly—or getting treatment and getting right back in there to finish?

Maybe you won't win this particular race, but you can still give it your all. And with the same determination, you may win the next one.

# HERMANISM #46

## ANYBODY BEEN DIVORCED TWICE ... WHO SAYS WE LEARN FROM THE FIRST BURNING?

We all know someone whose marriage has failed. More than half of us have experienced it firsthand. Some people get divorced once and say never again. Others get remarried and divorced again and again. Are these people impossible to live with or just having a hard time finding love? If their last marriage is a great one, does that mean they learned something from their earlier relationships? Were they worth all the pain? Or are these people just stupid for trying again?

We are all human, flawed in many ways. Hardheaded. Every winter, the news reports are full of stories about mountain climbers lost in a storm. There's been an avalanche. Or the visibility got so bad the climbers fell into a ravine. Every year it happens. And every year more climbers head up the mountain, daring death to take them.

Talk about daring death. Evel Knievel broke over a hundred bones in his body and still kept doing his stunts. And then his son Robbie followed in his footsteps. We may think the Knievels are a little crazy, but we can't help but admire their commitment.

Entrepreneurs are action junkies too. They want to build something. Or start something. Or take over something. They don't always follow the rules. And they don't always succeed on the first try. Hell, their hardheadedness, their limited knowledge, and their willingness to take chances where others won't almost guarantee they will fail, sometimes over and over again. And for this reason, the business action junkies are responsible for many of society's advances—through their repeated failures.

My first marriage failed. My metal stamping business lost hundreds of thousands of dollars. When I ran for public office, I was thousands of votes from respectability, let alone from winning. The car dealership I started with a friend was called L&H Auto and was quickly nicknamed Laurel and Hardy. My assorted failures literally added up to millions of dollars in losses.

In subsequent years, my brokerage firm, which consulted with financially troubled companies, billed out many millions of dollars in fees. The companies I helped sell were able to keep thousands of workers employed. My family's bed and breakfast and fine dining restaurant was profitable and won national acclaim. The previous paragraph makes me sound like a complete failure; this one, a huge success.

It's like I tell my kids all the time: **If you do a lot of things, you will make a lot of mistakes. But you will also do a lot of things right.**

# HERMANISM #47

## IT SEEMS THAT THOSE WHO "WORK SMARTER" ALSO PUT IN MORE HOURS.

Over the years of owning many companies and consulting with hundreds more, I have been in direct contact with probably about 80,000 workers. Everyone from dishwashers to drivers. Cooks to CEOs. Bankers, lawyers, judges, accountants, factory workers. All kinds of workers.

I have seen workers who come to work late. Take off early because of a headache. Enjoy long lunches. Go on extended vacations. "Pace themselves."

But those workers were not the successful ones. The successful ones put in more hours and worked smarter than everyone else around them. Without exception.

To "work smarter" is a concept that you need to understand. It means not making sales calls at lunch time or in the late afternoon. It means not waiting until the last minute to plan a strategy. To work smarter means thinking of ways to achieve your goals more efficiently. Finding a way to get more done in a day than your competitor does. Or a way to get more done with fewer people. Or less expensive equipment.

It always seems to come back to time. How can you find the time to get more planning done than you already do? To do more research, read more. To process the data from a meeting and come up with answers that others do not. What do the really successful people do to find that time?

For one thing, they set the alarm clock earlier.

People who are enthusiastic about building their business or expanding their career—from stockbrokers to athletes—usually get up before the rooster. Their heads are spinning with ideas that need to be worked out. The solitude of the morning hours, sitting alone at home or in an office or running in the dark—that solitude is an elixir. Ask successful people and most will say they love the alone time that jump-starts the day. (And while those individuals whose workday begins in the evening might not get up at 5 A.M., they still find that alone time to get ahead.)

Because the next thing you know, other workers show up to distract you. The day fills up with meetings and other "stuff." Phone calls to answer and customers to attend to. Anyone who believes there will be enough time in the regular workday to come up with the next big idea will never really succeed—because the workday is crushed with everyday stuff. *Minutiae.* Look it up. And don't let it get in your way.

Simply put, successful people work longer hours. How committed are you to succeeding?

By its sixth year, my brokerage firm had achieved a very high level of success. New leads were coming in every week from would-be clients. We were handling cases all over the country, selling and restructuring large companies—companies doing millions of dollars in business that had run into financial difficulties and had to be sold to recover money for the creditors. But we didn't liquidate those companies. We found buyers who took them over and continued to run them. In short, we sold "dogs with fleas." And in my firm, I was the best at selling those dogs.

In one particular year, we earned $2 million in commission fees. Of that $2 million, 55% came from the deals I closed; the other 45% came from deals closed by the other eight partners.

Why was I so much more successful than my partners? For one thing, because I had been in the business longer and had more contacts giving me leads. Prior success gave me an edge. Was I smarter than the other eight guys? My editor won't let me say what I might really think, so let's just say probably not. Was I just luckier than they were? Poppycock.

As a business, we wanted to know why I was doing so much better than all the other partners—and what they could do to improve. So we decided to take a look at the numbers. (If you haven't realized it yet, I am a numbers guy. I believe in numbers as if God Himself came down and told me to do so. Numbers tell us everything, if we pay attention.)

In front of a conference room full of my partners, I stood at the chalkboard. I pulled out my calendar where I had recorded all my daily activities and wrote up the numbers I had tallied. The numbers from the twelve months when I kicked their asses in fees.

These deals I did were all over America, in many different states. So the first number on the board was daily travel time: six hours per day. Six hours of every day, traveling to or from a courthouse appointment or a meeting with a factory owner or banker or lawyer or potential buyer.

I had records of over two hundred takeoffs and landings that year. That is a lot of air travel. And the places I went were not usually across the street from the airport, so I spent a lot of time in rental cars and trains as well. All in all, I averaged six hours of the day just getting from here to there.

And what did I do when I got there? I averaged one two-hour in-person meeting per day. That doesn't mean I saw one person every day. Sometimes I saw two in one day and none the next. But my average was one meeting that lasted two hours, for every workday of that year.

And how did I communicate with all those bankers, lawyers, owners, and buyers in the days before text messaging and e-mail? I spent four hours a day on the telephone. In the early 1990s, before cell phones became part of the human anatomy, we sat in an office, picked up a receiver, and dialed. My telephone bill for that year was just under $10,000. Four hours of every workday jabbering about stuff. Sometimes screaming, other times appeasing. Sometimes getting new information, sometimes sharing information. Four hours of every workday that year.

And one last number. Another six. That year, I averaged six working days a week, not the typical five.

As I stood in front of this room full of bright, energetic, success wannabes, I added up the numbers. **Six days a week of work, six hours a day of travel, two hours a day in meetings, and four hours a day on the telephone. More than two hundred flights and a hundred nights that I didn't make it home.**

That is how I had beaten the rest of the partners in fees.

The room was very quiet. Didn't anyone have anything to say? Finally, one partner in the back raised his hand. "Yes?" I called to him.

"We aren't going to do that!"

The rest of the partners in the room burst out laughing. Then the questions began: "How can you stand doing that? What about family time? When do you see your friends?"

They thought I was nuts. They all agreed that something had to be wrong with me—because they didn't want to do what I did, and they didn't want to look bad.

What is your excuse for not working more hours?

# HERMANISM #48

---

**⅓ THINK THEY HAVE NO PROBLEM.**
**⅓ ARE PARALYZED.**
**⅓ WANT OUT AND MOVE ON.**

---

This Hermanism describes the thousand owners in trouble that I visited over the years.

Some owners are like ostriches. They bury their heads in the sand. I have talked with owners who owed millions in debt, were 120 days late on their accounts payables, and couldn't price an order correctly—and they still looked at me like I was crazy when I said they should sell and get out.

What was I talking about? They had no problem. Hell, the company had lived on this precarious edge for years. This time was no different from any of the other bad spells. It would all be over soon. After all, they had always recovered before.

**Do you have a problem?**

If you own a business, ask yourself these questions:

+ Do you have enough money in the bank to pay one month's worth of bills?

+ Are your sales going up or down?

+ How are your margins?

+ Is your bank considering pulling your line of credit?

If you don't own a business—and we all do really, we are all a "business" of a sort—then check your bank balance against your credit card debt. Are you living over your head?

Here's a common problem that's often overlooked. With low interest rates, many homebuyers choose an ARM, an adjustable rate mortgage. As in, your interest rate started at 4%, but now that the economy is changing, your rate is going to 6%. That's a 2% increase in your mortgage rate. Big deal, right? But that 2% rate increase equals a 50% increase in the amount of interest you are paying. Still think it's not a problem?

Have you identified a problem with your business or your personal finances, but don't know how to fix it? Are you so emotionally drained that you feel like you can't move? **Are you paralyzed?**

The most successful businesses recognize when they have a problem and do something about it, quickly. Whether it's to a new strategy or a completely new venture, they move on.

WORTH THE PAIN 189

# HERMANISM #49

## ASK ANY PERSON WHO HAS SUCCEEDED IF IT WAS WORTH THE PAIN.

Success is like any other high in life. It is a rush. It may be as simple as getting the closest parking space. Ahhh, that little rush of victory. And all it took was driving around the lot three times.

Naturally, bigger goals get a bigger rush. They also usually require more pain.

But succeeding at something makes the pain seem unimportant. If that were not true, would women ever have a second child? They know the birth will be painful, and still they want to bring that second life into the world. As a father, I am grateful for that. After all, the births don't cause men any pain. (We feel the pain later, when those babies have grown into moody teenagers.)

As sports fans, we celebrate when our team wins the pennant. But we can't possibly feel as good as the players do—because we didn't experience the pain it took to get there. I have never heard a winning athlete say, "It wasn't worth it. The practices were too hard. I was away from my family

too much. Keep the trophy. I don't want it." No.
They cry, they leap into the air, they blow kisses,
and team members hug each other at the sheer
exhilaration of that winning moment.

**At the moment of success, we forget the cost.**

Do we ever go too far? Or pay too high a price
attempting to succeed? You bet we do. Because
we are flawed and sometimes ignore things we
shouldn't. Relationships, for example. Any joy in
a success after a break-up will be tempered by the
loss. But there will still be joy.

The ideal is to achieve success without paying too
high of a price. The person who figures that out
gets the biggest rush in the end.

# HERMANISM #50

## THE MOST BITTER PART OF FAILURE IS QUESTIONING YOUR OWN EFFORT.

You can't control everyone else's actions, but you are accountable for your own. So give it your best.

I have spent a lot of time and money on deals that I didn't get. So what? I knew that I had done all I could, and I believed that, over time, the numbers would come back my way. My effort would pay off.

Let's say you know the sales closing rate is one out of three and you make $100,000 per deal. If your goal is to make $1 million, then you better go see over thirty prospects. Visit twenty-two instead of thirty and a funny thing may happen. You may go six for twenty-two. And you may have gone four for eight on your next eight calls.

Businesses fail for all sorts of reasons, many beyond our control. But if you don't put forth the effort and do everything you can to make yours succeed, the only person you can blame is yourself. And the bitter taste of "If only I had …" may last a long, long time.

# HERMANISM #51

## IT IS WHAT IT IS.

Pilot training is excellent business training. You must focus on the problem, and not let your emotions get in the way. After all, if you don't fix the problem soon enough, you could die.

It was my first night flight after returning from pilot training. I was preparing to fly about a hundred miles from the base to do a training exercise and then return to the base. Alone. At the last minute, a visiting pilot asked if he could ride along. He wanted to log a few hours in the air.

We had a full load of fuel. Adding my companion's body weight to the equation, we were too heavy. So we left our parachutes at the base. Without any chitchat, I took off and flew south. And then, over the Chesapeake Bay, we developed engine troubles.

I did what the textbook had told me to do. I called in the emergency and started to fly north, back toward the base. I was offered the option of heading over to what is now BWI Airport, several miles inland from the water we were then flying over. If we crash landed in the bay, we might both get out and no one on the ground would be hurt. But if we flew over land, more people could get hurt.

Which brings me to a lesson we had drilled in our heads during pilot training. What if you were trying to land in an emergency and you hit a schoolhouse full of kids? One instructor answered this way: "If God didn't want airplanes to crash land on schoolhouses full of kids, He wouldn't build schools on the ground."

It is what it is. **You can't ignore an action because of what might happen. You have to give yourself the best chance at solving the problem.**

Back to the night flight from hell. Knowing we were losing altitude with only one working engine, I looked north to the Chesapeake Bay Bridge and wondered if we could get over it and still make the base. The water was mighty dark down there. The guy on the radio said they were waiting for me at BWI—which meant flying a few miles over the many houses down there in the dark.

By now, my passenger, who had nothing to do but contemplate our doom, was showing his nervousness. And he chose that moment to tell me more about himself.

Seems he was an FAA crash inspector. He said our plane could be scattered in a lot of backyards after taking off a few roofs. He apparently had seen this happen many times. Those awful details had never crossed my mind, not until then.

But I continued to do what I was trained to do. I followed the checklist. I could see the airport ahead and the blinking lights of the fire trucks along the side of the runway. There was one last issue to overcome: the engine that had quit supplied the power to lower the landing gear. We would have to crank the gear down by hand. So what. That was in the book too, and I had memorized the book.

As that crippled airplane rolled onto the runway, I didn't have any real sense of impending death. I had merely experienced an emergency that my training had said might happen and had prepared me for. I had done exactly what I was supposed to do to overcome the problem.

I was young, naïve, and fresh out of pilot training, where I was led to believe that I was invincible … if I followed the book. My training had provided me with responses to help me overcome problems. Those responses wouldn't always work perfectly, but following their steps would give me the best chance of survival.

Thirty-five years later, those Air Force emergency rules are still burned into my brain. And they apply to a failing business as much as they apply to an airplane with engine problems:

| Failing Airplane | Failing Business |
|---|---|
| 1. Identify the problem | Identify the problem |
| 2. Maintain aircraft control | Steady the business |
| 3. Land (eject if needed) as soon as practical | Safely exit the business |

Stop worrying about what being in debt up to your ass is doing to your life or your business. And concentrate on fixing the problem. On getting out of debt.

Stop bullshitting yourself that everything will be okay because you are a good person and nothing bad could happen to you. Recognize that you have a problem. And act on it.

If your business is in catastrophic failure, do not crash with it. Get out alive somehow. Because wishing it were not a problem doesn't make it not a problem. **It is what it is.**

# Hermanism #52

## Tiger Woods works the hardest of any golfer. Coincidence?

Even when he is ranked number one, Tiger Woods hits thousands of golf balls. Why? Because he wants to keep being the best.

Only when you are working harder than anyone else at your chosen endeavor will you be the best at it. If you don't want to work that hard, don't expect to be the best. And you have to keep working at it. Today your company may be very successful. Stop putting in the same amount of effort and see how long before the company falters.

There are no short cuts. None. Forget looking for them. Stop trying to figure out how to rest on your laurels and still be successful. Just get up every day and do the work. It's all about the effort.

When life is beating me up, I sometimes hear Ringo Starr's words ring in my head: "It don't come easy. You know it don't come easy. Got to pay your dues if you want to sing the blues, and you know it don't come easy."

# HERMANISM #53

## WHAT DID YOU DO TODAY TO MOVE THE BALL DOWN THE FIELD?

If, as the saying goes, a journey of a thousand miles begins with one step, and you want to finish the journey relatively quickly, then you better do some walking every day.

You may not need to go into the office every Saturday and Sunday, but you better spend some of your weekend thinking about what needs to be done or working on new ideas. Your competition is. If you want total freedom from work on your days off, you might be happier as an employee.

But don't confuse activity with progress. I know owners who work fourteen-hour days doing things they enjoy that don't get them anywhere. For example, if you like to tinker in the shop and make things, you might spend all day working on a new project. But are you getting closer to success if no one is working on bringing in money from your last great idea?

Do you ignore the stuff that has to happen to actually achieve success—the boring, grinding things that must be done every day to move the ball down the field? You must be disciplined enough to do what is necessary to move your business forward.

Fifty calls a day to find a new client—you hate picking up the phone, but if you skip the calls today, you better do one hundred tomorrow.

You need to work on the monthly budget, but you would rather see if you can make the machine run a little faster to get out more parts. (Sure, that's a valuable use of your time, but it can't take priority over what needs to be done today.) So you put off doing the budget and then wonder why you're overdrawn at the bank six weeks later.

Success requires attention to countless details. The things you like doing, and are good at, are among them. But unless you also do all of the other things, you will be running toward the sideline and not the goal line. (And if you like this metaphor, don't miss Hermanism #66.)

# HERMANISM #54

## WHEN YOU LOOK IN THE MIRROR, SEE WHAT'S THERE.

How many times do we fool ourselves with believing what we wish something were, rather than what it really is? We all do it—with our physical appearance, our relationships, our kids, our financial condition.

**Not facing the reality of a situation is a major cause of failure.** If you acknowledge a bad situation for what it really is, you can formulate a plan to either change the situation into a favorable one or recognize that it is time for you to move on, before further damage is done. If you don't, well ...

Not seeing the train about to crush you does not make it disappear. It just means you get run over without recognizing your impending doom. And you don't get the chance to jump off the tracks and save yourself.

Let's say you start a business and it loses over $100,000 in the first year. Ouch. Best case scenario: You had the money to sustain you through the loss. More likely scenario: You borrowed the money to cover your loss and now have an even bigger hill to climb.

Suppose you break even in your second year. If you were funding the business yourself, that means you didn't lose any more money. If you borrowed money to cover your first-year losses, you have to pay still more interest on that $100,000.

In your third year, you start to make a profit—let's say $50,000. This is progress. But when you see your remaining debt (or your still-substantial financial loss, if you're in the best-case scenario), you may wonder why you should keep going.

And in some situations, you may be better off getting out and finding a job where you would make a $50,000 salary without the headaches of business ownership, or debt, or risk of more failure. Jump off the tracks before the train gets to you.

In cold blunt terms, the person who finds out he has cancer and faces that reality has a much greater chance at recovery than the guy who steers clear of doctors and hospitals—and dies without ever knowing that cancer was eating him up inside.

# HERMANISM #55

## ARE YOU MAKING MONEY ...
## OR WASTING TIME?

If you own a business, people assume you are rich. "So and so must be raking it in. Have you seen their ads, heard their commercials?" "Did you hear they just got a new contract to sell such and such?"

Of course, you do need to maintain the appearance of success. Who wants to do business with someone who looks like a failure? I certainly couldn't make sales calls in a ten-year-old Datsun with rusted-out fenders. But I was anxiously awaiting those commission checks, because the payments on my impressive new ride were killing me.

I love the TV commercial where the guy is on his lawn mower, riding past the kids in the backyard pool, talking about the country club he belongs to, and showing off his beautiful new house. How does he do it? "I am in debt up to my eyeballs," he proclaims. "Can someone please help me?"

You can't wear a frayed suit and be taken seriously, but you can't afford Armani either. Be wary of how far you take the façade. Fess up. How much unnecessary fluff do you have around you just because you think it makes you look good?

The odds that your new startup company can afford a Mercedes are against you. Same for the beach condo. Because the first year or two of establishing your company usually drains your accounts. To make it to the finish line and be profitable, you have to sacrifice. Too often, owners aren't willing to give up their toys or appearances to allow their company enough breathing room to survive in the long term.

Tens of thousands of small-business owners are slaves to their companies. They never look at the hourly wage they make, because they know that working for someone else may pay more. They fight with their spouses because they are rarely home. They cheat their children out of precious family time. Their health takes a back seat to work demands.

Even the owners bringing in a half-decent revenue get trapped. Some call this the "golden handcuffs." The owners make just enough that they can't risk leaving. Or they feel like they can't give up the façade of success. They pay their bills and their employees, but it requires some serious juggling. Some continue doing this for years. Why?

**Because they won't face the reality that they are just wasting time and not really making money. They aren't getting ahead.**

Owners who have a business that fails completely may be better off than those who get trapped. How do they get out? What do they tell their friends? How do they face the truth that their dream isn't going to happen?

The courage it takes to leave (not quit) is perhaps harder to muster than the courage to start a new business. When you plowed ahead and "went for it," you expected huge success. When you make the decision to pull the plug, you are admitting you failed.

But is that really true? If you think so, then you better go back and read some of these Hermanisms again.

Money is only one measure of success. If, by leaving your company behind, you recover your health or your personal life, isn't that a win? If you have the courage to admit that the business wasn't meeting your goals, and probably wouldn't no matter what you tried, you can bask in the glow of success in what you learned from the experience.

It might hurt for a while to realize you didn't achieve all you set out to accomplish, but you can recover—and with a fresh start, use what you learned to move closer to the success you desire.

# HERMANISM #56

## FAILING BUILDS CHARACTER, EVEN IF "NOBODY NEEDS THIS MUCH CHARACTER."

Little kids want to win. And sometimes they will cheat to win. The same temptation exists in the world of adults. When things aren't going in our favor, we are often faced with an "easy way out." Resisting the temptation to cheat, lie, steal, or do some other dastardly act to win takes character.

All of the business owners I have visited in the last twenty years were losing money. Their livelihood was disappearing, the business that they had put years of sweat and pain into. But they didn't all react in the same way to their misfortune.

Some told me they didn't care if they screwed the vendors out of money. After all, the vendors had made millions off them over the years. Others made comments like this: "I don't care if I fuck the banks out of their money. They make millions; this is all I have." They seemed to forget that when they borrowed the money from the bank, they had promised to pay it back.

Some owners looked me in the eye and said right away, "What can we do to save the jobs? What do I have to do to make this right?" But there weren't very many of those.

Most people fell somewhere in between. They struggled with the ethical dilemma of saving themselves versus doing what was best, what was right, for the other people involved.

**Our character is revealed when we are challenged, not when all is well. When we fail, not when we succeed.**

If you find yourself in a tough spot, think it through. Do you cave in for an "easy" win, or do you show character and keep struggling through? Either way, you'll have to live with the consequences.

## HERMANISM #57

### IF ONLY GOLD MEDALS COUNT, ARE ALL OTHER OLYMPIANS FAILURES?

I have been a baseball fan my whole life. I always hope my team wins, but I know they can't win every year. In fact, if the only thing that brought me happiness was first place, I would give up the team quickly—they don't finish in first very often. What I really enjoy is the pursuit of first place.

In the Olympics, athletes that win first place receive a gold medal. But months ahead of the actual games, to get a chance at the medals, they have to make it through the trials. Most athletes train for years before they even qualify for the trials. They spend years working toward one goal: a gold medal. Hundreds of athletes all over the world want it, but only one can win.

Some young athletes burn out early for one simple reason. We are teaching them the wrong goal. Of course, we need to teach them to win. But not everyone can win. The real goal in sports should be to enjoy the game and its challenges while you are working for that win.

So when I watch the Olympics, I hate it that the commentators miss the point of all those years of hard work when someone gets a second, third, or, God forbid, fourth place. Fourth place is the worst: so close, but the athlete gets nothing.

I think the announcers need to stop saying how crushing it must be to come that far and not win a medal. I think they should talk more about how wonderful it must be to be there at all. To have made it to the Olympic games. They should acknowledge that being an Olympian is one of the greatest accomplishments any athlete can achieve.

I am not going mushy. Of course, we all want to win. So kick yourself in the ass and go all out after first place. But when a swimmer expected to win every race he enters only wins five out of six and is asked how disappointed he feels, I am enraged. Why should he be disappointed? He just won five freaking races against the greatest swimmers in the world. What is disappointing is that we focus so much on winning that we miss out on all the other success stories.

Being a great athlete should be the goal. Doing your best. Winning is just the cherry on the cupcake.

How does this apply to business? To me, business is like the Olympics.

There may very well be someone better than you at what you do. A vital customer might bail out on you and cause you to fail. Your machinery might break down at the wrong moment. To be the best in your field, many things have to go your way. You can't control many of those things. But you can control yourself.

So, did you try your best?

If you put forth your best effort and finished fourth, you should feel the joy of knowing you are participating on a level that you strived for. And you can feel proud that you have given it your all.

And you can continue to love playing the game.

# HERMANISM #58

## YOU WOULDN'T BE READING THIS IF YOU DIDN'T WANT TO BE BETTER.

Thanks for picking up my book.

And congratulations.

You wouldn't have gotten this far in the book unless you were trying to learn something. That means you already realize the importance of taking advantage of every type of education you can.

Keep those antennae up.

You may have an opportunity to meet a person with more experience than you, or at least a different experience. Newspapers, magazines, books, TV shows—information that could help you is all around. Suck up as much of it as you can.

**You can bet your competitor is studying, reading, watching, and listening to try to get ahead. You would be wise to do the same.**

# HERMANISM #59

## IF THE CUSTOMER WANTS VANILLA, QUIT TRYING TO SELL HIM CHOCOLATE.

Pay attention. This may be the best sales lesson you ever get.

**I believe a sale is made in the first ten minutes. And I believe the sale is made because the customer buys the salesman, not the product.** Of course, you must have something the customer wants or he wouldn't have given you the appointment. But you couldn't possibly know what it is that the customer specifically wants when you walk in the door.

So do yourself a favor. Speak for about four minutes to show your personal credentials. Then spend another minute to mention something that you have noticed about his business. Then, and here's the key, ask him what he wants. In the next five minutes, if you listen attentively and he likes you, you will get the sale.

It's that simple.

During all my years in sales, the number one mistake I saw salesmen make was not giving the customer what he wanted. They were so in love with their product, or their pitch for the product, that all they cared about was telling the customer what they wanted to tell him. And selling him something they were sure he needed. The fact is, even if the customer desperately needs your product, if he doesn't like you, he will find someone else to sell it to him.

All companies give their salesmen a pitch to deliver. I never started mine until my ten minutes were up. The customer had to buy me first and then the product. If he didn't want to buy from me, then sitting there all day pitching him the product wouldn't close the deal.

You cannot close every pitch with an order. Every customer walking in the store won't buy something. But you can always leave the customer feeling okay about not buying something—if he feels like you listened. And you didn't try to sell him something he didn't want. And you may get a sale from him the next time.

So many salesmen go in armed to the teeth with product knowledge, ready to overcome objection after objection. They know how to bring the customer back to their side every time, how to dazzle him with brilliance. In fact, they almost humiliate the customer—what a fool he would be if he didn't see the advantages of their product.

Bad idea. The amount of times you will write an order by wearing a customer down will never be enough to overcome the bad will you have created by not letting up on those customers who outlasted you. They won't ever have you back, and they may not let your company in the door again.

Hit enough front doors, make enough presentations, and follow my simple plan, and you will be the top salesman in the company. Remember, you got in the customer's door because he needs what you have. So let him tell you exactly what he wants and tailor your pitch to what he says. You will close the sale.

Forget the pitch. Forget that chocolate is on special this month. When a customer tells me he wants vanilla six minutes after I arrive, I write his order for vanilla and head out the door. He likes me. I just gave him what he wants. I didn't try to unload on him the other stuff I wanted to sell. **I let him present his problem, and solved it for him.** And my closing average was consistently higher than the other salesmen's at every company I ever worked for. Give the customer what he wants.

# HERMANISM #60

## A GREAT IDEA, TALENT, HARD WORK, GOOD TIMING, HELP FROM OTHERS, IMMENSE PUBLICITY, AND LUCK ARE SOMETIMES ALL YOU NEED TO MAKE IT.

Easy Street—we're all looking for it. And an easy way to get there would be nice too.

My friend Arnie buys lottery tickets every week. He swears it is his birthright: he will soon win the millions he yearns for and slide into his golden years flush with cash. Fortunately he also continues to work hard every day. Because the reality is that Arnie will almost certainly need that paycheck to keep a roof over his head and food on his table. Lottery tickets notwithstanding.

Luck alone usually isn't enough to make someone successful. Obvious, I know; we see the lottery odds every day. But less obvious may be the fact that a great idea, talent, and hard work sometimes don't cut it either.

Some people open a new business thinking that their idea is so good that people will beat a path to their door and riches won't be far behind. Glorious success. Simple. While a good idea is the foundation for success, many good ideas have been born and have died without anyone else ever knowing they existed.

Success depends on a lot of factors coming together: some of those factors are within our control, some aren't. Like the timing of world events, the launch of competing products, knowing so-and-so who knows the president of such-and-such company.

**All you can do is all you can do.** Do everything within your power to make your idea succeed. Work as hard as you possibly can. Pursue every avenue you can think of to give your idea the chance it deserves. And if you still don't succeed, don't beat yourself up: some things just aren't meant to be.

# HERMANISM #61

## IT'S A MARATHON, NOT A SPRINT.

Time is an ever-present issue in our lives. It seems we all want more time, to live longer—because we have more things that we want to do. More things to accomplish. And we realize we need time to do that. So why is it that so many people think that financial success should happen overnight?

Every success takes time to create. If you think you will get rich quick, forget it.

Did you finish school in a few months? No, it took years. Did your kids pop out of the womb already knowing about life? No, it took them years to learn. Succeeding in business is no different. It may take years. Years.

Remember when you were a little kid, riding in the family car? Getting to the park or the zoo or Grandma's house seemed to take forever. But after a few rides, you realized you weren't going to just materialize somewhere else. You were going to have to spend the time in between here and there. You decided to make the most of it. So you looked out the window or read a book or poked and prodded your little brother. The trip itself became an experience, no longer just a means to an end.

My youngest daughter, Shannon, is full of great ideas. When she was little, one of her ideas was the "big hand theory." She wished that when she got in our car, a big hand would immediately pick up the car and put it down at our destination. The trip would be over in an instant. Shannon and I still talk about her big hand theory and about what we would miss along the way if we didn't actually experience the journey.

Owning a business requires you to go on a journey. Success takes time, lots of time. Don't start a company thinking in six months you will be able to buy a new Jaguar.

Succeeding in business is like running a marathon. It requires commitment, a long and difficult training period, more hard work, and more pain. Then the starting gun sounds and you've got a very long road ahead of you.

# HERMANISM #62

## IS WHAT OTHERS SAY AN "OFF RAMP" OR AN "ON RAMP" TO YOUR LIFE'S HIGHWAY?

I often seem to be headed toward places that others can't see. When I look down the road ahead of me, I may see hazard signs, potholes, and creaky bridges to cross, but at the end, I see success that's worth the danger. If I listened to what others said all the time, I would get so distracted by those obstacles that I'd abandon my journey altogether.

Some people are "skeptators," skeptical spectators who are always trying to discourage your dreams. When I started my first book project, the editors said not to expect too much success. Publishers said they wouldn't print so many copies of an unknown author's book. The printer thought I had lost my mind when I told him I wanted ten thousand copies right off the bat. Even the book distributor questioned the number of books we were shipping to his warehouse, afraid one day he'd have to throw them away.

But at the end of my highway, I could see huge demand for my material. After all, I understand concepts that hundreds of thousands of business owners need to know. And my stories are interesting to other people too, people who are curious as to how some of my axioms might apply to their life. I had to trust my vision—while still considering the valuable input I got from other people.

Some professionals (lawyers and accountants, for example) tend to be very conservative. They don't want to advise their clients to take a large risk. They would rather see a client not try and not fail, then try and maybe fail. By following their safe strategy, you may give up the potential for greater success.

When listening to others, you need to be selective. Choose to hear only the good things and you will fail—by ignoring some critical realities. Listen to only the naysayers and you will never do anything. Sift through the rhetoric. Determine what is based in reality and what is based in fear or ignorance. Consider people's area of expertise and their understanding of your goal.

The professionals I encountered with my book projects advised me within their vision of what I was trying to do—which was not necessarily the same as my vision. Realizing that, I considered their input but didn't let it hold me back.

Follow your vision and stay on your own highway. If it leads to failure, at least you can say you followed your own path.

# HERMANISM #63

## KNOW IT WILL BREAK.
## KNOW IT WON'T BE DELIVERED ON TIME.
## KNOW IT WILL COST MORE. AND KNOW
## HOW TO MAKE IT WORK ANYWAY.

You already know Murphy's Law: Anything that can go wrong will go wrong. But perhaps you haven't considered that the principle behind this seemingly negative outlook is really a positive one. Because if you truly live by Murphy's Law, you are prepared for the worst and you are confident that you can handle it.

To be successful, you need to live in the positive world of knowing that no matter what bad thing happens, your business can weather the storm—because you are ready for the storm. Because you built in an extra day for production. Because you scheduled the work properly even if time was tight. Because you calculated the cost for the fact that some raw materials would have to be wasted.

**Anyone who thinks strictly at the edge of positive possibility can almost certainly count on failure.**

Let me illustrate.

My first business was an office services company: we answered telephones and did copying and mailing tasks for other businesses. One time, I had a chance to bid on sending out the tax bills for a large county in Maryland.

The job was simple: take the bills that had been prepared by the county, put them in envelopes, seal the envelopes, stamp the envelopes, sort the envelopes by zip codes, and deliver them to the post office on a certain date.

It was about fifty-five thousand pieces of mail. No problem. My sorter did X pieces per hour: it stuffed, sealed, and stamped. I bid the deal based on the best possible performance of my equipment. Nothing would go wrong, and I would make a sweet profit. I bid and got the job.

I quickly realized my first mistake. Have you ever seen fifty-five thousand pieces of mail? There were so many freaking boxes of bills and empty envelopes that they took up more square footage than we occupied. My staff was incredulous. How could we work with all these boxes piled up in our faces? How could we move around to get the bills into the sorter and into the envelopes when there was no work area left?

And the sorter. It was like a kiddy version, a home office version that handled fifty bills at a time—not fifty-five thousand. What was I thinking?

I recruited friends and family for a "mailing party." Everyone, fold these bills. Now, let's get them in the envelopes. Oh, and did I mention that we have a legal deadline for mailing them out?

People were in my living room, dining room, and kitchen starting at about 6 P.M. (the earliest they could get there after their regular workday). And we didn't quit all night. The clock was ticking. We still had to sort by zip codes so we could get the postal rate reduction that I had included in the bid.

People were getting grouchy. I was nuts: it was now a unanimous decision. What the hell kind of businessman was I anyway, trying to do something this impossible? "And, by the way, Herman, you are paying us. In real money, not just the pizza and Cokes you put out for us to eat."

I didn't even have a vehicle big enough to carry the bags to the post office. It took me several trips.

In the end, the client got his project completed. The county residents got their tax bills. The people who helped me got paid—and lost some sleep. And I lost my ass.

Bid something wrong and you will pay for it.

Figure out your real costs, including potential setbacks—or you will subsidize your clients' work. And they won't even thank you.

# HERMANISM #64

## ANSWER THE PHONE AS IF IT WERE A GUEST AT YOUR FRONT DOOR.

I am always amazed when I call a company and the person answering the telephone chirps out, "Blah blah blah, please hold." And then there's either silence or music, while I sit and wait.

Would you open the front door at your place of business, see that it is a customer, and then, without letting him speak, ask him to wait a minute and slam the door in his face? While he stands outside the door contemplating what to do, it may occur to him that he is coming at a bad time and perhaps he should go away. Wouldn't he feel better if he were let inside and shown to a waiting area until you have time to meet with him?

I would much rather get your voice mail than have you jabber quickly and disappear, while I dangle on the line, hoping you will come back before it's time for my next appointment.

And when I am next in line in your store, why do you shun me so you can take a call from someone who wants to know if you have a size six of such-

and-such in yellow? You jabber with this person who may never spend a cent on your merchandise, while I stand there in front of you, trying to give you my money.

**Enough with the multitasking. Give me your undivided attention long enough for us to conduct our business—or I will get the message that I am unimportant.** Is the call you answer going to get you a better deal? Is that guy you put me on hold for worth more to you than I am?

Choose your duty. Answer the phone or wait on the live people in front of you; don't try to do both. And then treat every one of those people with respect. If I am standing or sitting in front of you, then let your voice mail work. That's why it was invented. To let callers get through and begin the process of doing business when you aren't available. They have voice mail; they know how to use it.

Your phone system even lets you tell those callers, "I am on the phone or away from my desk right now; please leave a message, and I will get right back to you." So, if I'm the caller, I have already learned that you are in and will get my message and that you will call me back. I can ask my questions or leave information to move our business forward. And even if you get my voice mail when you return my call, you can give me the answers I need. Boom. Progress has been made.

But for God's sake, slow down when you are leaving me your number. And say the numbers without chewing peanut butter while you talk.

On the other hand, if you actually take my call and we're having a conversation, would you mind letting the next call go to voice mail? Must you "place me on a brief hold" while you jump to another possibly "more important" call? Let's finish our business as if we were the only two people alive. That way, I feel you are paying attention to my needs as a customer and you feel I care about your business. Civil, isn't it.

If you are the switchboard operator or the equivalent at your business, perhaps you should let the caller know right away, "I am here alone and may have to answer other calls." As the previous owner of various small businesses, I do understand that situation sometimes comes up.

But most of you are not in that situation. You are merely grazing through calls, looking for the best one. Take them one at a time, and let your voice mail work the way it was intended.

# Hermanism #65

## PLAN FOR SUCCESS, NOT FAILURE.

Here's an example of this Hermanism in action:

You own a restaurant and are looking at the reservations for tomorrow night. You have six tables reserved, a total of eighteen guests. You look at the schedule and figure two servers can handle that workload. So you give the other three servers the night off to save yourself some labor cost.

What you don't realize is that a concert scheduled for the symphony center across the street will bring in a crowd. The concert was not on the normal schedule. Different people will be attending it, not the usual ticket subscribers who know how to make reservations at your place. And most of the concert-goers will be in the age and income bracket you target. Someone had even mentioned the concert to you, but you weren't familiar with the artist, so you didn't link it to any rush of business.

And when tomorrow comes, lo and behold, guests without reservations are swarming, looking for dinner before the concert. The place is packed, just like you always wanted. And the guests are young and hip and have pockets full of sweet plastic to order fine wines with that wonderful menu.

You have plenty of tables for them, but not enough waitstaff. And you haven't prepped enough food for eighty guests. You've prepared for thirty, based on your reservations and the normal amount of walk-ins on a non-symphony night.

The scene is a nightmare. Hey, where is my food? Hello?! Can we get our order taken over here? Your two servers are busting their asses, but there's no way they can keep everyone happy. And so the service is a "goatfuck" (an old military word describing a very ugly situation).

All because you failed to plan for success—by having five servers on duty and plenty of food prepped. You planned for failure and ended up with a disaster.

Not only was the dining experience a bad one for these guests. They are the type to text message the disaster to their friends while they're waiting for their food, then e-mail other friends the next day, and, for good measure, go online and post a bad review of the restaurant—all to retaliate for not getting their dinner in time before the concert.

You can't ever apologize enough to win over those guests who came in unannounced and had a horrible experience. And you can't undo the bad PR they put out there, so you've lost out on other potential guests.

**Plan for success.** Schedule staff as though a full house will arrive. Prep enough food to overcome an onslaught. If the onslaught doesn't arrive by a certain hour, let some of the servers go home early.

Don't miss out on a chance to succeed just because you think it's unlikely to happen.

# HERMANISM #66

## MOVING FORWARD IS BETTER THAN MOVING SIDEWAYS. STAYING IN ONE SPOT WEARS A HOLE IN THE CARPET.

Watch an NFL game and you'll hear the announcers talk about a running back moving east and west instead of north and south. The running back who cuts right sideways for five yards and then spins around and runs back across the field ten yards, then jukes back three more to the right and then gets tackled hasn't gained eighteen yards. He is tackled right where he started. And now he's tired from all that running.

Every day I ask myself Hermanism #53: What did you do today to move the ball down the field? I know I did a lot of things hoping to make progress. But did I actually move the ball farther toward the goal line or just wear myself out running sideways?

Keep in mind that you are trying to achieve a goal. All activity is not necessarily progress toward that goal. Failing to recognize that fact can eat away at your business like a hole in the carpet.

Many professionals have worked in my brokerage business over the years: hard-working men who were successful at other ventures before joining our firm. They came to work early. They made hundreds of calls every day. Some made many trips to see clients. They did research at night. They were always doing something. But some of them never made any money. They never signed up any deals or closed any deals while they were with us. They were running sideways.

It costs your business money to have Mr. Whirlwind of Activity make all those calls and trips. If he isn't scoring any goals, he is drilling you into the ground financially.

When I brought some of those guys into the office after months of this unproductive activity, they were shocked that I recommended they leave.

"C'mon, Herman, I work harder than most of the others here. I put in more time than at least half of these guys."

In some cases, they were right.

But business doesn't always reward activity; it rewards results. Business, unlike today's peewee soccer, keeps score. And you need to do the same.

Because, at the end of the day, results are all that count in business.

Find a way to measure every activity of your business. In every department. Every piece of equipment. Because if running that equipment or having that salesman isn't getting the ball farther down the field toward your goal, you need to change it before there's irreparable damage.

And for any of you reading this who may be feeling sorry for the guys we let go, remember this isn't a social work book; it's a business book. And making good business decisions allowed us to make bigger profits. And pay more taxes. To support more social programs to help those in need.

# HERMANISM #67

## NOT LETTING GO WHEN IT'S OVER
## IS LIKE STAYING IN A BURNING BUILDING.

Almost every owner I have met who was losing money had stayed too long. I did the same thing myself in the company I turned into a publicly trading entity. Many owners make this mistake. They stay too long and as a result sometimes go down with the ship.

Once you realize that you are going backwards, any hesitation to shift your efforts to saving yourself will cost you.

Say the smoke alarm goes off in your house. It does what it is supposed to do: it warns you that there is danger. You then have a choice. You can leave immediately and save yourself, or you can start going through your jewelry to decide which pieces are worth saving. They better be worth a lot because you may pay with your life. Heed the warning, and you live to buy more jewelry. Hesitate when the warning sounds, and you may never wear jewelry again.

Business can burn you. Say you have invested $200,000 in a company. And it is barely staying afloat. You are working for very little money, sometimes taking home next to nothing so you can pay the business bills. Your numbers are your alarm.

Should you ignore the warning, take out more credit card debt, and plow ahead? Should you make a financially life-threatening situation even worse?

**You had better heed Hermanism #21: Know math or no money. You had better study the numbers and decide if now is the time to exit. Before you get badly burned.**

# HERMANISM #68

**I ONCE FINISHED A RACE AND DROPPED TO MY KNEES, HURLING. A MAN TOLD ME NOT TO TAKE LOSING SO HARD. I HAD ACTUALLY WON THE RACE.**

It was high school. I was a senior, and I was fast. My speed made me not bad at lacrosse, good at soccer, and very good at track. Each year, there was a one-mile race to determine the fastest runner in the school. I had won the year before, and I figured repeating the victory as a senior would be a breeze.

Then I learned that this year's race would have a different twist. The freshmen and sophomores were getting a headstart. Seems the person in charge of the race thought those younger runners didn't have the physical maturity of the juniors and seniors, so they "deserved" a fifteen-second headstart. What?! That would give them a one-hundred-yard advantage.

The older runners plotted their strategy. Not on how to win the race, but how to cut into the fifteen-second headstart. We had to show we were faster than the freshmen and sophomores somehow. No one thought we could actually catch them and win.

Except for me. I drew the course on a napkin. I said if we caught the younger kids by the halfway point, maybe we would psyche them out and be able to hold them off and win the race. The other guys thought I was nuts. "You would have to sprint full out to catch them in half a mile. And then you'd be so tired, you couldn't finish the race at that pace." I wasn't convinced.

Race day came. Boom. The starting gun went off. Juniors and seniors stood their ground while the freshmen and sophomores took off. Fifteen seconds seemed like an eternity. Those little bastards were way off in the distance. C'mon, dammit, shoot the gun off again. Finally. Boom.

I took off as if it were a hundred-yard dash. And I didn't slow down. I passed many of the younger guys, and I soon saw something wonderful: the kid in the lead. We were getting to the halfway point, and I had caught up despite their headstart. But that guy stayed shoulder to shoulder with me for the next quarter of a mile. Man, why didn't he fade?

As we made the final turn for home, I kept telling myself that my plan had worked. That I was going to win. All I had to do was stay ahead of this one guy and I would still be the fastest guy in school. And because my confidence was soaring, I flew up the last hill and won by several strides. And then I collapsed.

It wasn't pretty. I was sick, very sick. And so fucking happy that I didn't care. As I knelt on the ground, hurling as if I had been out all night drinking, a teacher came over to see if I was okay. He leaned over me and told me that it didn't matter if I had lost; I had worked hard to finish. Still on all fours, I looked up and proudly told him that I had not lost; I had just won the race. It is forty years later, and I still remember that feeling. Despite the pain, and perhaps partly because of it, the winning was glorious.

What person over forty doesn't remember watching "the thrill of victory and the agony of defeat" every Saturday afternoon with Jim McKay and the Wide World of Sports? In the opening, when the man swooshing at breakneck speed down the ski jump missed the landing and crashed painfully? Week after week after week, that guy fell—a reminder that excelling at sports requires commitment, despite all the pain.

My first year of Little League baseball, our team lost every game but one, which we tied. But something lucky happened that year. Every team sent two kids to the all-star game. Because our team was so bad, I made the all-star team. On any other team in the league, I would have never gotten that chance.

I was certainly no all-star. One Little League season, I never got a hit. Not one. I went an entire freaking season of about twenty games without ever getting a hit. Two years later, I hit over .400 and played first base for a championship team. **With sports, I learned that you get another chance to succeed.**

There is something about us that makes us enjoy winning. Cave drawings depict competitions and the glory of victory. Today, we play checkers and video games. We bowl. We play tennis and golf. We watch football, baseball, and hockey, and we love it when our team wins—as if we had won the game ourselves. We're glued to reality TV, wanting to see who will win. We watch the stock market and bet our savings on who will win.

But we also recognize that we have more to gain by competing than money or trophies or game balls. As we challenge ourselves, we learn a lot about who we are. And we get enormous satisfaction out of trying to win—even when we don't.

Losing stings; never playing stings worse. Get in the game.

# HERMANISM #69

## WHAT ARE YOU TRYING TO DO, AND WHAT ARE YOU REALLY DOING?

You tell yourself you are just trying to make a living. You are just doing what is best for your family. You are doing the best you can to earn money for your children's future.

But there are many other things you are doing too. You are staying within the law: drug dealers make more money than you do. You are trying to keep your dignity: strippers in a men's club take home more cash than you do. You are being your own boss: many employees have better retirement funds than you do.

Sure, money is a driving force for everyone who works. But other factors come into play when you step out of the box and decide to own and operate your own business. As a business owner, you take on duties that employees don't have.

People in the restaurant business have told me many times that "if you want to make a small fortune in the restaurant business, you must start with a large fortune. And you will end up with a small one." If 95% of restaurants fail, don't tell me you are opening a new one just to make money. It's nineteen to one against you that you will succeed at that goal.

People start companies all the time without ever examining the total sum of the reasons they are doing it. And because they don't acknowledge why they are doing it, they sometimes get stuck in a business that isn't making them happy. Even if it is making money.

A few years ago, we bought a restaurant with a bed and breakfast so our son, a world-class chef, could have his own place. So he and his wife could make their living hosting guests at the inn and serving his wonderful cuisine. My wife and I did not buy the place to spend our days doing paperwork and answering phones.

But the place was too much for just my son and his wife to operate. To be successful, other family members had to get involved. That wasn't in the plan. But we did it—to support our son until his goals were achieved.

He proved his talent. He received accolades and wonderful job offers from resorts all over the world. They wanted his cooking skills and he would not have to manage the property. Others would do the parts of the business he didn't want to do. He no longer needed our restaurant.

The family members that had supported his needs could move on to other phases of their lives. And because the business had been profitable, they all got a small stake to finance their next ventures.

"Why would you sell such a wonderful business that was making money?" people ask.

**Because making money was not our only goal. The other goals had been achieved, and we were ready to do something else.**

# HERMANISM #70

## THERE IS NEVER ENOUGH TIME TO LAUGH WITH YOUR KIDS.

I have often thought that by trying so hard to succeed, I have lost out on the greatest gift life gives us: time with our children. This Hermanism is for my kids.

I have sacrificed many hours of laughter with my children—so I could succeed and hopefully make their lives a little easier. So they could spend more time laughing with their kids.

I learned this from my father. When I finally got some precious alone time with him, I asked, "Why do you work so hard, Dad?" He always replied so I wouldn't have to work so hard in "the salt mine," like he did. He wanted me to have it easier.

And I thought if he was willing to make that sacrifice and show me his love in that way, I wanted to do the same for my kids. Because I loved my father more than anyone else and wanted to be just like him.

Finding the right balance between spending time trying to be successful and spending time with your kids is a challenge—one that I may have sometimes failed at. All I can say in my defense is my intentions were good.

# HERMANISM #71

## IF SUCCESS FELT GOOD TO YOU, STOP WALLOWING IN THE FEELINGS OF FAILURE AND MAKE YOURSELF SUCCESSFUL AGAIN.

I was alone. I had just closed the doors on the business that I had been sure would make me a rich man. Three years earlier, I had started the company with $15,000 and an idea. I had watched it grow to a national sensation. And then flop.

No more Dallas morning talk show. No more Florida TV appearances about how the company would take the country by storm. No more radio interviews. It was all gone. No more money. No more employees. No more customers. No more paychecks. And debt piled so high there was no daylight to be seen. Jesus, it hurt.

Whether you run a hundred-million-dollar business or drive an ice cream truck, if your business fails, you will know how I felt. Faced with that kind of pain, a lot of people start drinking. Some do drugs. Some chase women. Many wallow in self-pity. But none of those things get them any closer to success.

**Here's the important thing to remember: you survived. And survivors get another chance.** Think of the race car driver who survives a devastating crash. He is hurt and suffers through months of physical therapy. When his body has healed, he has a choice to make: (a) never risk another high-speed crash and give up on the thrill of racing or (b) get back out there and risk it all again to do what he loves.

Breathe in. Breathe out. Your business is gone. You are broke. People may think terrible things about you. But your legs work. And so do your arms. And when you take a walk in the park, people say hello and don't realize what a failure you are. You're not wearing a letter, scarlet or otherwise.

Say this to yourself every day: **I can wallow in self-pity, or I can begin to heal. I enjoyed the feeling of success, and this feeling of failure sucks.**

Even if you become a dishwasher after being a bank president, you can feel the success of being the best dishwasher. Or the best shoe salesman. No, you might not go out and immediately become CEO of your next venture. But you can start right away to seek success and put the failure far behind you.

It takes thick skin and enormous self-esteem to convince yourself that you will be okay. You might even need some outside help. But remember that you did many things right to get as far as you did. And if you worked as hard as you could and still failed, so what.

Chasing success and that wonderful feeling of accomplishment took effort every day. And you can put forth that same effort again. Wallowing in self-pity and the feeling of defeat just makes it that much longer before you will feel good again.

# HERMANISM #72

## SOMETIMES WE HAVE TO TRUST WHAT WE CAN'T SEE.

Moses tapped his stick on the rock and out came water. He had faith. There are countless times that you need to trust what you can't see. The Air Force gave me a great example of this.

As a pilot, you are taught that the instruments will get you safely from here to there, even when you can't see three feet in front of you. You can overcome the weather by using what the instruments tell you. Trust them and you will be okay. So, in pilot training, after you are comfortable taking off and flying in a straight line and descending for a landing when you can see, you have to learn how to do the same things when you can't see.

So as not to lose a bunch of airplanes in the process, the Air Force used Link trainers to help new pilots learn this skill. Flight simulators. They're awesome. You act just like you're flying a real plane, and the movie screen in front of you shows you what you would see from a real cockpit. And so you practice your flight skills on the ground.

Then one day, after you take off, the movie screen goes gray, like a blinding snowstorm. But you keep flying. Your instruments tell you how high you are. How fast you are going. What direction you are heading. And the controller on your headset talks to you just like when you are in the real airplane flying in the real sky. You check your gyroscope to see if your wings are level. Your radio signals give you your headings, and a mileage figure shows how far you are from a marker on the ground.

After I had a few of these blind training sessions, my flight instructor and I strapped ourselves into a supersonic jet, the kind that could break the sound barrier. The instructor, sitting behind me, wished me luck. As we taxied down the runway in Phoenix, Arizona, my nerves flared up a little. **Faith, baby, have faith.**

Almost as soon as we lifted off the ground, the instructor told me to "get in the bag." That meant pull the hood over my head and attach it to the dashboard so I couldn't see out of the airplane. Not at all. This was just a few hundred feet after liftoff in Phoenix.

Then the instructor said, "Take me to Los Angeles." The rest was up to me.

I called the tower for instructions and was told to climb to so-and-so altitude and then turn to such-and-such a heading. No sweat. Now fly to a certain point on the ground at that altitude using just your instruments to guide you. Just like in the Link trainer—except that we were thirty thousand feet in the air and going about four hundred miles an hour.

According to the coordinates I had calculated when we made the flight plan, I hit certain ground points and made the correct turns without ever seeing outside of the plane. I had faith in the instruments.

Finally came the approach. Descend and maintain such-and-such an altitude. Turn left and head such-and-such a heading. You are now over the outer marker. Begin your descent for landing. The lights blinking indicated we were two miles from landing. The instructor told me to pull back the bag.

I was on a perfect glide slope to land. And the runway was right there in front of me. I pulled back the throttle and slightly on the stick and landed. Touchdown in Los Angeles. Hundreds of miles from Phoenix. Without seeing a thing.

Plan your business. Know where you want to go. Make a road map with mileposts to check your progress. Know what you should be doing at certain points in the future to reach your goal. Know what signs to rely on. And while you are in a real-life shit-storm, when you can't see for looking, trust your road map to guide you home.

# HERMANISM #73

## WHAT YOU LEARN MAY BE WORTH MORE THAN WHAT YOU MAKE.

New businesses aren't created from nothing. They usually build on something we already have—with an idea about to how to make that something better or sell it to more people.

You can look at pretty much any new business as the next step on a long walk. iPods didn't pop out of nowhere. They came from the continuum of vinyl, eight tracks, cassettes, and CDs—and our desire to have more stuff in a more convenient package. Day spas were once barber shops. Nordstrom was in days gone by an open air market.

Building the better mousetrap is what most business progress is about. Once in a while, the guys who make an "original" product, like a Hula-Hoop or Slinky, zoom out in front with what becomes the recognized brand and then stick around for a long time, making them very rich.

But there are tens of thousands of business ventures that never make any real money. Most of us think we will be more successful than we actually become because we think we are offering something new. We find it hard to accept that we are not that different from the next guy. A dry cleaners is a dry cleaners is a dry cleaners. Your dress shop sells the same thing as hundreds of other dress shops. Restaurants are on every corner—and they open and close so fast that our curiosity for trying new ones always has a ready supply.

So when you start a company that really is just like many others and you find yourself tired of working all day every day and not really getting ahead, just stop and think about what you are learning.

Before you started the company, maybe you didn't have any experience in planning a budget. Or making a payroll. Or ordering supplies. Or knowing what to carry in inventory.

While you may not have made any real money yet, you have just graduated from another class in life. And you'll be that much better prepared for the next term.

# Hermanism #74

## Waiting for others to do it your way takes forever.

We have all heard this saying at some point in our lives: if you want something done right, do it yourself. Let me give it a slightly different spin. If you want something done your way, do it yourself.

Working at a business with my wife and our children has been one of the joys of my life. But it has also been one of the hardest things I've ever done.

My wife is one of the smartest people I have ever met. Our children are smart. We are all overachievers. So why did I often find myself saying, "How can you all be so wrong?"

It's not that they were wrong. They had their own visions, their own ideas about what should be done, and they weren't always the same as my ideas.

If you expect others to do it the way you want it done, you will be disappointed almost every time. In fact, waiting for others to see it exactly your way and to do it exactly your way will take forever.

So if you want the work done in a certain way, be prepared to do much of it yourself—or it will never get done.

# HERMANISM #75

## IF YOU REALLY DON'T LIKE
## WHAT YOU'RE DOING, STOP DOING IT.

When you hire new salespeople, they start out full of enthusiasm. They can't wait to set the world on fire. Some bolt out of the gate so fast that you're sure they will break all the company records.

A few months later, they're spent, deflated. They miss their sales targets. Commissions aren't pouring in. The travel is harder than they expected. They don't like what they are doing, and they won't ever like doing it. The best thing you can do is let them go. Cut the ties.

People who own a business are different in many ways from others. Not better, just different. They like something about the process of owning a business—whether it is starting one up, helping it mature, or running it after it reaches some level of success. But sometimes they stop liking it—not because it is hard or the cash flow gets tight. They grow to hate the everyday stuff they must do to keep the business going.

I am a great deal-maker. Correction. I was a great deal-maker. I could look at a business, analyze what needed to happen, and negotiate with bankers, lawyers, owners, and buyers—and in a reasonably short time, get a deal done. I did that for almost twenty years and made a very good living.

I loved it. The challenges of obtaining the deal. Working with owners resistant to the reality of their situation. Getting creditors to support a plan. Negotiating with CEOs who wanted to buy what we were selling. Touring plants with prospects. But then, after all those years and all those meetings and all those successes, I didn't like it anymore.

The travel started to bug me. The owners seemed so unrealistic. And where did they find these new young bankers who think they know everything? In one of my last meetings, I started to outline what the company needed. The banker interrupted me. He wasn't interested in hearing what I had to say; he had already decided what the deal needed.

When I asked him how many deals he had completed, he said three. "Wouldn't you like to hear the thoughts of a guy who has done three hundred?" Apparently not. When did I become a dinosaur?

I didn't like fighting back anymore. So I walked away. And I don't do deals anymore.

It's not a lack of energy. It's not that the work has become too challenging. And for sure it is not because I already have enough money. It's just not what I like to do anymore. And so I've moved on to something else.

Writing books is my new challenge. I accept it. I will have to travel to sell these books. Let's go. It may be tough to be a successful author and make money at it. Bring it on. Because I like doing this. I have a new dream energizing me. And I hope I like it long enough to be as successful as I plan to be.

# HERMANISM #76

## READING IS THE MOST PAINLESS WAY TO LEARN.

In the United States, we all have free access to information to help us succeed at whatever we want to do. We can learn just about anything without spending a cent.

Just go to the library and pick up a book. There are books of all kinds out there. Hundreds of thousands of books. Books about cats and dogs. Flying. Baseball. War. How to make widgets. There are books on virtually everything mankind has ever done.

Really think about this for a minute. Tens of millions of human beings have tried all sorts of things in all sorts of ways—and you can read all about it without leaving your hometown. Walk into your library, and it is like walking into a town square where people are lined up to teach you all that they know. For free. At your own pace.

Sure, now there are the Internet and educational television and DVDs. They're all helpful.

But there is something comfortable to me about reading a book. It is one on one. The writers speak directly to me. As fast or as slowly as I want them to speak. I can read ten pages and shut off the conversation, or I can listen for twenty more pages. I can read some today and none tomorrow. The story, what the writer wants me to know, will still be there when I pick it up again.

You can learn about cooking without turning on the stove. About the oil business before investing a dollar. You can learn how people accomplished things, without spending the years of effort they did.

Don't get me wrong. You can't learn everything from a book. But you can speed up your progress if you have a great deal of book knowledge before you start to actually try something.

Movies are wonderful resources for learning too. But the moviemaker is telling you a story about someone else who did something. Likewise, teachers tell their students about people who have accomplished great things.

Give me a book written by the guy who actually did the great things, and I am spellbound.

You don't just get what he did. You also get his adrenalin, what he felt at both the high and the low spots.

Didn't you feel yourself flying under the hood when you read about my "blind" flight to Los Angeles? And yet, you may have never set foot in a cockpit. Didn't you share the joy (and the pain) of my victory when I won the race in high school? Only the person who did it can really tell you what it felt like.

Give your kids books. Make them start reading. Soon they'll love it. All the readers I know cherish the quiet hours they spend with a book.

You are alone when you read. It's just you, thinking about the words of the writer. Just like you are alone running a business or making a decision. If you can think your way through a book, you can think your way through a difficult decision.

**P.S.  Most leaders are readers.**

# HERMANISM #77

## MAKE THE RIGHT BUSINESS DECISION REGARDLESS OF MONEY.

The cornerstone to my brokerage business was trust. The seller, the buyer, the banker, and the lawyers all had to trust the deal. They had to believe it was in each of their best interests to complete the transaction, or the deal wouldn't close. No closing meant no fee. Not good for business. So building that trust was a critical component of getting over the finish line.

In almost every deal we did, the players were in different states. These companies were doing business with customers all over the country, if not the world. The banker that made the loan was in another state. The buyer's business was several states away. To get all the players in the same room at the same time required a lot of travel.

And guess who did the most traveling? The broker. We might be in three cities in two days having individual meetings, just so we could be face-to-face when we shared information. Why be face-to-face and not just talk on the phone? Trust.

When you are willing to get on an airplane and rent a car or take a cab to someone's office to tell him the same thing you could say on the phone, it builds trust. What you have to say is important enough to share in person. When you look the person in the eye, it seems to mean more.

How do I know? Because when I didn't make the flights and tried to save the cost of a trip, deals didn't close as often. Squabbles developed over minor issues. You've probably experienced this yourself. Discuss a problem on the phone and it's easy to hang up without solving the problem. Get face-to-face and you're more likely to resolve it.

After making this mistake a few times, I learned to make the trips. Spend the money and the time to resolve the issues. And I closed more deals. But the newer partners tried to save a buck and a day away from family by conducting multimillion-dollar deals on the phone. And it cost our firm plenty of money.

One guy lost a $100,000 fee on a deal because he didn't visit a banker. The partner had never been face-to-face with that banker. He didn't want to spend the $800 to see the guy for ten minutes to say what he could say on the telephone. And the banker didn't trust him enough to take the buyer's offer.

You face decisions every day. Do I really have the money to advertise? Should I get that machine repaired when we are already broke? Is this the time to buy more inventory, when we're already late on our bills?

My suggestion is a simple one. Ignore the reality of your financial condition for a minute. **What should you do if money were no object? That is what you should do.**

If you can't run your business by doing what is right, regardless of your financial condition, then you are probably swirling near the drain.

## Now go make something happen!

Reading this book should have jarred something inside of you. A desire to move forward with your idea. A belief that you can overcome the obstacles that will appear. That you won't allow failure to destroy you.

If you're unsure about what to do next, write about your situation. Writing can help you gain a better perspective and will often jog thoughts free to help you figure out your next move.

You can also **e-mail me at Herman@hsbpress.com**. Tell me about your idea and what you plan to do next. I would love to dialogue with you. Throughout this book, I have said that you can learn something from people who have had different experiences than you. I do not have all the answers. But I will gladly offer my point of view and challenge you with some blunt input.

If your college, book club, or business organization needs a speaker, **give me a call at 410-453-0280**. I love sharing the stuff life has taught me. Lessons often learned the hard way. Lessons from bankers, lawyers, and business leaders that helped me succeed—and can help you too.

And by the way, if you haven't already done so, read *The Innkeeper Tales* to get the full Herman story.

# HERMANISMS

# A Note About Statistics

Numbers regarding business in the United States often vary depending on the population criteria, the means of collection and interpretation, etc. Below I've noted the source data on which I based my statements:

[1] 2004 U.S. Census: 5,782,199 small businesses (with fewer than 100 employees)

[2] 2003 U.S. Census: 572,900 startups; 554,800 businesses that filed final returns or simply disappeared

[3] Study for Wells Fargo/NFIB Series on Business Starts and Stops, based on a Gallup poll of 36,000 households per year (1995–1998): 39% of businesses were profitable, 30% broke even, and 30% lost money

[4] Small Business Administration May 2002 report, *Small Business by the Numbers*: 66% of businesses with employees were still operating 2 years after startup; at 4 years, the survival rate fell to 49.6%; at 6 years, it was only 39.5%